DORRT INFORMATION SERVICES

P9-DNX-483

DATE DUE

OC 03 '97		
NO 19 '97		

Demco, Inc. 38-293

After the War

After the War

Jean Bruce

Fitzhenry & Whiteside
in cooperation with the
Multiculturalism Directorate, Secretary of State
and the
Canadian Government Publishing Centre,
Supply and Services Canada

© Minister of Supply and Services Canada, 1982.

Publishing Centre Catalogue No. Ci48-1/1981E

No part of this publication may be reproduced in any form, or by any means, without permission in writing from the publisher.

Fitzhenry & Whiteside Limited
150 Lesmill Road
Don Mills, Ontario, Canada M3B 2T5

Canadian Cataloguing in Publication Data

After the War
Bibliography: p.
ISBN 0-88902-587-8
1. Canada - Emigration and immigration - Biography.
2. Canada - Emigration and immigration.   3. Canada - History — 1945-1965.*   I. Bruce, Jean, 1936-

FC613.14A47   304.8'71'0922   C82-095139-0
F1034.2A47

Printed in Canada

Typesetting: Jay Tee Graphics Ltd.
Offset Lithography: Imprimerie Gagné

Thanks to the Ontario Arts Council and the Canada Council in the production of this book.

Contents

Picture Credits

The following sources of illustrations are gratefully acknowledged.

Air Canada: 111

Alcan Ltd.: 142

Archdiocese Chancery Office, Toronto: 169

Archives of Saskatchewan: 162

Brown, H. A.: 120, 179

Canadian Lutheran World Relief: 39

Canadian Pacific: 31, 41, 97, 113

Canadian Press: 21

CN: 2, 20, 26, 40, 43, 48, 60, 90, 99, 100, 101, 102, 109, 113, 114, 115

Conference of Mennonites in Canada: 37

Department of National Defence Collection, P.A.C.: 13(pA112367), 19(PS112368)

Dickmanis, A. K.: 47, 147

Glenbow-Alberta Institute: 25, 49, 51

International Refugee Organization: 29

Jewish Immigrant Aid Services: 52, 159

Kramolc, Ted: 28, 35

Montreal Gazette, Montreal, P.A.C.: 31(PA115767), 141(PA115765)

Multicultural Historical Society of Ontario: 36, 42, 53, 106, 112, 129

N.F.B. Multimedia 9, 10, 38, 59, 61, 62, 65, 67, 69, 71, 73, 74, 75, 76, 77, 78, 79, 80, 82, 84, 85, 86, 87, 88, 102, 103, 121, 128, 131, 133, 135, 144, 145, 146, 152, 155, 156, 163, 164, 166, 171, 172, 187

N.F.B. Multimedia, Malak: 57, 66, 70, 72, 83, 181

Negro Community Centre, Montreal: 119

Ng, Nancy: 108

Ontario Archives: 63, 89, 92, 93, 104, 123

Ontario Hydro: 57

Public Archives of Canada: 17(C27645), 33(PA111595), 45(C53923), 54(PA113910), 56(PA111590), 68(PA111584), 81(PA121405), 97(PA111585), 98(PA111579), 105(C47282), 117(PA110924), 118(A112798), 125(PA112366), 127(PA111591), 130(PA111592), 139(PA111582), 141(PA111581), 143(PA111580), 151(PA111567), 151(PA111566), 153(PA115633), 173(PA112793), 183(PA115632)

Sisters Service of Mary Immaculate: 50

Sturhahn, Rev. William: 154

Toronto Telegram: 27, 32, 34, 44, 46, 94, 111, 136, 177, 188

Toronto Transit Commission: 137

University of New Brunswick: 149

University of Newfoundland: 157

Anonymous: 148, 165

Preface

WELL OVER A MILLION IMMIGRANTS came to Canada in the ten years after the Second World War. This period, 1945-1955, was the bridge between today's urban, industrial, heterogeneous society and the Canada of earlier times: a country of family farms and primary industries, of small cities and smaller towns. A country whose population was largely divided into two basic groups: those of French origin and those of British ancestry, and whose administrative traditions were British Colonial.

In the photographs advertising postwar Canada to prospective immigrants, the old Canada and the new were frequently presented side by side: the horse-drawn plough and the latest tractor; the woodstove and the electric range; the one-room schoolhouse and the consolidated school; the house-proud mother of a family and the working woman; the country store and the city supermarkets and department stores.

In the late 1940s and early 1950s, the Immigration Branch could still tell would-be immigrants that "agriculture is Canada's largest industry," although the era of cheap, accessible land in "the last best west" had long passed. It was a period when unskilled immigrant labour was still in great demand, as it had been earlier in the century, to work on the farms, in the forests, down the mines, on the railways and in the construction industry. It was also a time when racial discrimination was still a major feature of Canadian immigration policy, when frank preference was shown for British, northwest European and American immigrants, as it had been thirty years earlier.

This book is about the people who came to Canada in the aftermath of the Second World War: the warbrides, the British, the Dutch farm families, the Americans; the refugees and displaced persons from central and eastern Europe and the Baltic states (known as "DPs," despite belated government efforts to call them "New Canadians"); the former "enemy aliens," Germans, Italians and Japanese; the sprinkling of French, Belgians and Scandinavians; the first Chinese to be admitted after a twenty-four year ban; and a wide range of others who were admitted in small numbers, including Indians and Pakistanis, blacks from the Caribbean and North Africans.

Over 50% of these postwar immigrants went to Ontario, and close to 20% to Quebec. More people went to British Columbia and the prairie provinces than to the Atlantic region, but some immigrants went to every province, and almost 250 of them talked to me about what it was like to come to Canada in those years. So this book is not only about the people themselves, but about the kind of society they came to.

"After the war" was a phrase which came up so often in conversations with postwar immigrants that it seemed to be a natural title for a book about them.

For Harold, Dora and Gordon,
who came after the War.

I   Setting the Scene

TO WOULD-BE EMIGRANTS from war-weary Britain and battle-scarred Europe, postwar Canada looked like a promised land. Reassuringly remote from the battlefields of World War Two and the menace of Russian advances during the "cold war" era, Canada appeared to be a very good place to start a new life. While the United States was the first choice of many people, neighbouring Canada came a close second.

As the Second World War ended, however, the Canadian people and their government showed no immediate desire to open the doors to large numbers of immigrants. The government's first priority was the adjustment from a wartime to a peacetime economy. One million Canadian men and women who had been employed in war industries had to find other work, and 975,000 members of the Canadian armed forces had to be absorbed into the postwar labour force. 48,000 servicemen had married overseas, and their wives, together with 22,000 children, arrived in Canada between 1944 and 1946.

These natural concerns with postwar readjustment, in a country whose population was less than twelve million, were strengthened by Canadian memories of conditions after the First World War, when wartime prosperity had been quickly followed by recession. Thousands of people could not find work, and the social unrest which developed culminated in the Winnipeg General Strike of 1919. It seemed possible that history might repeat itself.

In 1944, Canadians were also aware that wartime prosperity had been preceded by massive unemployment in the 1930s. Many people who had suffered during the Depression feared that harsh economic conditions would return, sooner or later. The pervading sense of insecurity among Canadian workers was remarked upon by various immigrants who arrived in the late 1940s. "You talked to ordinary people and they didn't believe their luck, that they had a job," one Austrian immigrant told me. "It made me very impatient because, after Europe, things looked so good here. But they were still afraid of the Depression, and the fear was in their bones."

The reluctance of many Canadian workers to have the doors opened to immigrants was shared by various young, professional people, for different reasons. Their careers had been hampered by the Depression and then by the war, and they did not welcome competition at the point when they were at last establishing themselves.

A third reason for the Canadian public's mixed feelings about immigration was a long-standing "anti-foreign" attitude which had influenced Canadian immigration policy since the nineteenth century, when immigrants were divided into "preferred" and "non-preferred" groups. "Preferred" immigrants were those who came from Britain and the United States, closely followed by northwest Europeans. Central, eastern and southern Europeans were "non-preferred," and Jews, orientals and blacks came at the bottom of the ladder.

Background

At the turn of the century, Laurier's minister responsible for immigration, Clifford Sifton, had stood out against this approach, arguing that "stalwart peasants in sheepskin coats" were much more likely to succeed in breaking new land on the prairies than the traditional British immigrants, who were increasingly urbanised. The campaign for settlers, launched during Sifton's time, brought hundreds of thousands of newcomers to Canada, and between 1896 and 1914 over three million arrived. Sifton left the Cabinet in 1905, but his successors under Laurier and Borden tried to encourage immigrants from "preferred" rather than "non-preferred" sources. But their efforts at selection were overwhelmed by the momentum of this first, great wave of immigration.

The First World War brought an end to the flood of immigrants, and in the early 1920s, the Canadian government began to restrict entry to Canada. Those on the bottom rungs of the ladder were the first affected. The Chinese Immigration Act of 1923 effectively cut off Chinese immigration, and relatives of Chinese residents of Canada were denied entry. In 1928, before the onset of the Depression, eastern European immigration was cut back by two-thirds, and, once the Depression set in, immigration generally came to a near halt. Between 1931 and 1940, only 158,562 newcomers arrived, compared to 1,230,202 in the 1920s. Moreover, when R. B. Bennett was Prime Minister, from 1930-1935, the Conservative government deported 28,000 destitute immigrants.

As the importance of immigration declined, so did the department which handled it. Bennett's successor, Mackenzie King, abolished the Department of Immigration and Colonization in 1936. The Immigration Branch became part of the Department of Mines and Resources, and it remained there until 1951.

In the 1930s, apart from British subjects and Americans, only those European immigrants with enough capital to establish and maintain themselves on farms were admitted to Canada. So, with very few exceptions, the door was effectively barred to thousands of non-agricultural Europeans, and particularly Jews, who were desperate to escape the growing menace of Hitler's Germany.

The immigration policy of that day has been branded — and documented — as racist and inhumane by scholars Gerald E. Dirks, Irving Abella and Harold Troper. A longtime Liberal politician, and later Minister of Immigration, J. W. Pickersgill, told me that government policy when he first came to Ottawa in the late 1930s was "basically anti-foreign," and that, "regrettably," it reflected the public opinion of the day. The effects of heavy unemployment reinforced Canadian antipathy towards "foreigners." In the immediate pre-war years, racism, bolstered by economic considerations, overwhelmed the humanitarian protests of groups like the Canadian National Committee on Refugees.

The racial prejudice which permeated Canadian policy at that time was widespread among western nations. Xenophobia, as immigration specialist Freda Hawkins pointed out to me, was "an international syndrome" in the inter-war years, and immigration policies in the United States and Australia reflected the same prejudices, the same fierce hostilities and anxieties.

Returning Canadian troops aboard the *SS Louis Pasteur*, Halifax, June 1945. 557,000 members of the Armed Forces were discharged in the eight months after the war ended, and a further 175,000 were released the following year. The need to absorb so many veterans into peacetime jobs in a country of under 12,000,000 helped delay the development of a postwar immigration policy.

Quebec

In Quebec, opposition to postwar immigration surfaced before the war ended. In 1944, the Quebec Legislative Assembly passed a resolution threatening to boycott any postwar schemes of mass immigration. 1944 was also the year of the "conscription crisis," and the year when Maurice Duplessis' Union Nationale party returned to power on a wave of "anti-Anglais" feeling.

Quebec's antipathy to large-scale immigration dated back to the great wave of early twentieth-century immigration into the prairie provinces, which altered the balance of Confederation and Quebec's place within it. Only a small minority of newcomers were French-speaking, and even those from metropolitan France were treated with suspicion, as coming from an anti-clerical, republican society. Whatever their background, newcomers tended to be assimilated into the English-speaking community. In the opinion of many French Canadians, immigration was an English Canadian policy designed to counteract the effects of Quebec's high birthrate, and to ensure the predominance of the English-speaking population. Quebec's opposition was one important factor which delayed the development of a vigorous postwar immigration policy. After weathering the 1944 conscription crisis, Mackenzie King was convinced that concessions had to be made to Quebec opinion in order to preserve national unity.

Canadian Public Opinion

In Canada as a whole, public opinion about immigration was divided. In April 1946, when the Gallup Poll asked Canadians if they favoured large-scale immigration from Britain in the next few years, 45% were opposed (in Quebec the percentage was 76%) and only 37% were in favour. To the accompanying question, did they favour a large number of immigrants from Europe, 61% of Canadians (and 72% of Quebecers) said they were opposed.

Later that year, in October 1946, when Canadians were asked in another Gallup Poll which nationalities they would most like to keep out, the Japanese topped the list with 60%, followed by Jews with 49%, Germans with 34%, Russians with 31%, negroes (word used in Gallup Poll) 31%, Italians 25% and Chinese 24%. Even allowing for the fact that Canada had recently been at war with Germany, Japan and Italy, the poll revealed a continuing antipathy to "foreigners." Despite the influx of European settlers between 1896 and 1930, less than 20% of Canadians were of non-French or non-British origin. Slightly less than half the population were of British extraction, and almost a third were of French background.

As in the pre-war years, "anti-foreign" prejudice went hand in hand with economic uncertainty. In 1946, no one, least of all the cautious, aging Prime Minister, could be sure that Canada's wartime prosperity was more than a temporary phenomenon.

Labour Shortage

In 1946, despite the uncertainty about Canada's continuing prosperity, it was apparent that an acute labour shortage existed in Canada's primary industries: on the farms, in the forests, down the mines. In the war years, many of these jobs had been filled by government-directed labour: 11,000 Canadian conscientious objectors and 15,500 European prisoners of war. But conscientious objectors were released from agricultural work in August 1946, and, at the same time, prisoners of war were withdrawn from various work projects and sent back to Europe by the end of the year. Their departure posed a serious problem, since a Department of Labour survey of the labour force showed that few Canadians were willing to work at tough physical jobs in isolated areas. Immigrant labour appeared to be the answer.

As 1946 went by, other countries — notably Australia, Argentina and Brazil — began to recruit immigrant labour from Europe, and the demand grew for a review of Canada's highly restrictive immigration regulations and the formation of a new immigration policy to meet changed circumstances and postwar needs. Before the King government announced its broad policy, a series of Orders-in-Council were passed in 1946 and early 1947. They allowed four thousand Polish combatants to be brought to Canada to work in primary industries, and ''agriculturalists'' with sufficient means to farm were also admitted, along with those who were sponsored by relatives or by independent farmers. At this time, the door was opened to people with ensured employment in mining or lumbering and to dependent relatives of those Canadian citizens or residents in a position to receive and care for them.

Postwar Immigration Debate

These Orders-in-Council were passed while hearings on postwar immigration policy were being conducted by the Senate Standing Committee on Immigration and Labour. In the immediate postwar years, representatives of all interested parties, along with government officials from concerned departments and experts in the areas of population and natural resources, appeared before this Committee.

Foremost among the pro-immigration pressure groups were the industrialists and manufacturers and their spokesmen, the Canadian Manufacturers Association, and the Canadian Chamber of Commerce. Then there were the two railways, Canadian Pacific and Canadian National. Both still had agricultural land for sale, both still maintained their own departments of colonization, and both urgently needed labour to repair and maintain rail tracks across Canada. All these traditional advocates of immigration were joined by various ethnic groups, whose former compatriots — and, often, immediate families — were among the millions of refugees and displaced persons in postwar Europe. No official Canadian promise of help for these unfortunate people had been forthcoming by the fall of 1946, although the United States had announced its intentions in December 1945. Now, concerned ethnic organizations were, in turn, supported by various churches and humanitarian groups, like the Canadian National Committee on Refugees.

During the Senate Committee hearings, it became apparent that Canadian academic opinion was divided. On the one hand, geographer Griffith Taylor believed Canada had the resources to support 50 million people at current North American living standards, and Stephen Leacock, an economist as well as humourist, maintained the figure should be 100 million, "and below that I will not go." On the other hand, historian Arthur Lower, supported by Dominion Bureau of Statistics experts, argued that immigration in the past had made very little difference to the actual growth of Canadian society. One of the chief effects of past immigration had been to stimulate emigration to the United States, "the most attractive population magnet on earth," in Lower's words. "We get them from Europe, turn them into North Americans under our sun and on our soil, and then we lose them to the United States."

Lower's thesis was supported by figures given to the Senate Standing Committee on Immigration and Labour by the Dominion Statistician in 1946. Herbert Marshall showed that, between 1851 and 1941, 6,699,226 immigrants had entered Canada, and 6,301,320 people had left during the same period, resulting in an unimpressive net gain of 397,906. And according to the "displacement" theory of another academic, W. B. Hurd, it was native Canadians who were displaced by the inflow of newcomers. Since the United States had closed its doors to free immigration and established a "quota" system in the 1920s, new immigrants to Canada could no longer flow freely over the border, as they had done in the past. So they were the ones who stayed, while native-born Canadians left.

Despite these cautionary facts and figures, the Senate Committee on Immigration and Labour came out strongly in favour of a new and positive approach to immigration in the postwar era, as did the majority of witnesses appearing before it.

What was needed, said the Senate Committee in 1946, was "a new policy of selective attraction to replace that of repulsion." Both the Trades and Labour Congress (TLC) and the Canadian Congress of Labour (CLC), Canada's two main labour organizations, gave their cautious approval to this aim, provided that government, not private industry, controlled the selection, and provided that the system was designed to exclude certain groups. "It must be recognised that there are citizens of other countries who may be good brothers and sisters internationally, but yet would not be acceptable as brothers and sisters-in-law to Canadians," said Percy Bengough of the TLC. "Experience has clearly demonstrated that because of this fact certain nationals who have in the past been admitted into Canada remain as a distinct race and will remain a problem for generations . . . . Such people were a reservoir of cheap labour and a menace to Canadian standards of living."

No one at the Senate Committee hearings needed to ask Bengough whom he was referring to; they all understood that he meant Asians. And when A. R. Mosher of the CLC, and the Senate Committee itself, called for an end to racial discrimination in immigration policy, it was equally understood that everyone was referring to discrimination against certain European groups, and against Jews. Limitations on Asian immigrants were necessary because of the "problems of absorption," the Committee said. In 1946, Asians had not yet been given the right to vote in federal or British Columbian provincial elections, and they were still barred from certain professions, including law and pharmacy, in British Columbia.

Mackenzie King's Immigration Policy

The Senate Committee was enthusiastic in its reports on the need to admit substantial numbers of (European) workers, beginning as soon as possible. By contrast, Prime Minister Mackenzie King's impatiently-awaited policy statement, delivered in the House of Commons on May 1, 1947, was cautious and unenthusiastic.

King acknowledged Canada's need for a larger population. In the mid-1930s, the Canadian birthrate had sunk to a low of 20.1 per thousand, so the government was aware that there would be a shortage of young people entering the labour force in the early 1950s. Without immigrants, King said, there would be fewer than 13 million Canadians in 1951, and only just over 14.5 million in 1971. The Prime Minister recognised the "acute shortage of manpower" in Canada's primary industries, the need to develop natural resources, and to build a larger domestic market for Canadian manufacturers. Apart from all these reasons, a larger population was needed to defend Canada's huge territory in a time of international insecurity.

Those immigrants who were admitted would be selected with care and only according to Canada's absorptive capacity. Just how many that meant, said Mackenzie King, was impossible to predict with any degree of accuracy. In any case, immigration was a privilege, not a fundamental human right, and Canada was perfectly within her rights in selecting desirable future citizens.

British subjects and American citizens would continue to be given preference (France was added to the list in 1948 as a gesture to Quebec), providing they met certain standards of health and

Prime Minister Mackenzie King announced his government's postwar immigration policy in a cautiously-worded speech to the House of Commons on May 1, 1947. There was no Minister of Immigration in King's cabinet. Immigration had been drastically reduced during the Depression years of the 1930s, and in 1936 the Department of Immigration and Colonization was abolished. The Immigration Branch became part of the Department of Mines and Resources and remained there until 1950, when the St. Laurent government established a new Department of Citizenship and Immigration.

personal character, and could show they were unlikely to become public charges.

Next preference would be for the European relatives of Canadian residents, excluding German nationals who remained "enemy aliens" until 1950. "Some thousands" of the newcomers would be Europeans from the postwar refugee camps, because Canada recognised a moral obligation to help these people, although she was not committed to take a specific number, the Prime Minister said.

A limited number of other newcomers would be Chinese, because the government recognised the discriminatory nature of the 1923 Chinese Immigration Act, and this legislation would be repealed. Naturalised Canadian Chinese would now be allowed to bring in their wives and unmarried children, and so would East Indians legally resident in Canada, because they were British subjects. Both groups became eligible for Canadian citizenship on January 1, 1947, when the first Canadian citizenship certificates were issued. But the number of Asian immigrants would be strictly limited, because the government believed the Canadian people did not wish to make "a fundamental alteration in the character of the population. Large-scale immigration from the orient would change the fundamental composition of the Canadian population."

"With regard to the selection of immigrants, much has been said about discrimination," the Prime Minister continued. "I wish to make it quite clear that Canada is perfectly within her rights in selecting the persons whom we regard as desirable future citizens. It is not a 'fundamental human right' of an alien to enter Canada. It is a privilege."

Mackenzie King retired as prime minister in 1948, but his 1947 speech on immigration established the policy guidelines for the St. Laurent government and its new Department of Citizenship and Immigration. The new Immigration Act of 1952, which gave sweeping discretionary powers to the minister, embodied King's approach. Over the next few years, Walter Harris and J. W. Pickersgill, the St. Laurent ministers responsible for immigration, frequently referred to King's statements about "careful selection" and "absorptive capacity" and the "fundamental character of the Canadian people." However, the demand for immigrant labour was so strong that, during this period, selection was not as "careful" as was originally intended, Canada's "absorptive capacity" was very difficult to assess, and the "fundamental character" of the Canadian people changed significantly during the ten years after the war.

However reluctantly the door was opened by Mackenzie King in 1947, it swung wider under the pressure from employers in the buoyant years which followed the Second World War. In the ten years 1945-1955, over one million people were admitted to Canada, and the wave of postwar immigration was to continue into the 1960s.

Postwar immigrants came from diverse sources. The need for workers overrode Immigration Branch preferences for immigrants from traditional sources, as had happened fifty years before, during the first great wave of twentieth-century immigration. These newcomers changed the face of Canada, and the rest of this book is their story: why they came, how they got here, and what happened to them after their arrival.

II Welcome to Warbrides!

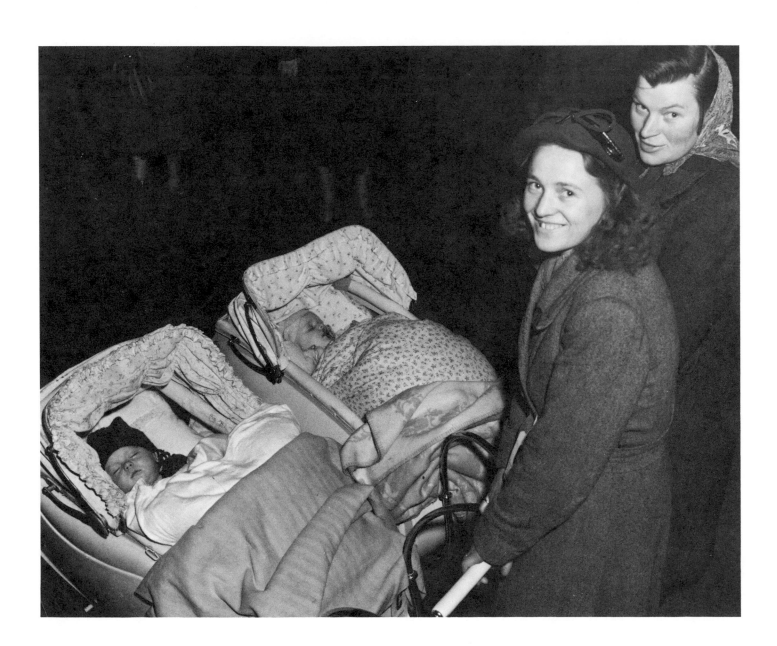

A Warm and Sincere Welcome

From the Atlantic to the Pacific in Canada a warm and sincere welcome awaits the girls whom Canadian fighting men have married in Britain. The people of Britain opened their hearts and homes to the boys of Canada's Armed Forces. You will find that the hearts and homes of the Canadian people are open to you.

You will be asked hundreds of times how you like Canada. If you can make your answer an enthusiastic "I love it!" you will make friends right and left. Canadians are deeply in love with their country — just as you are with your homeland. Some British people find the prairies drab and depressing at first, but the people who live on them have learned their beauty. Whatever you do, for the sake of your happiness, don't run down the part of the country you find yourself in, any more than you would criticise a meal in a friend's house.

Of course you will be lonely for your old friends and for your family, and homesick for your country at first. It's only natural that you should be and Canadians will understand and sympathise; but — don't make too open a display of it any more than you would display your personal troubles if you were still in Britain. Keep busy and interested, that's the best cure-all.

If you should unwittingly convey the impression that you regard Canada as in any way a dependency of Britain, you are likely to find that many people will temper their welcome with coolness. Canadians are proud that they stand on their own feet as a nation, that they have made their own declarations of war against the enemy countries, that they manage not only their own domestic affairs but also their foreign affairs . . .

Welcome to Warbrides, *Wartime Information Board booklet, Department of National Defence, 1944.*

British warbride re-united with her husband, Montreal. Of the 48,000 women who married Canadian servicemen overseas, 45,000 were British.

Welcome to Warbrides!

When you arrive in Canada in wartime from the United Kingdom you may, on the basis of your own first experience and observations, jump to the conclusion that your new home is a country that has been relatively little affected by the war. You will see cities brightly lighted at night. There will be a variety of foodstuffs such as you have not enjoyed for a long time. There will be very little noticeable sign of strain in the faces of the people.

But do not be deceived by that surface. Civilians in Britain were for many months under continuous and heavy direct enemy aerial attack, whereas Canadian civilians have had to gain their knowledge through reading and using their imaginations. But here are a few items of the Canadian war undertaking that might give you a better appreciation of what Canada has been doing in these years of war:

1. Of Canada's 11-1/2 million population, over 975,000 including 40,000 women have entered the armed forces. At the outbreak of war Canadian armed forces totalled only 10,200.
2. Canadian war industries are employing one million men and women, or about 10 per cent of the whole population. Canada is the fourth largest of the United Nations in producing war materials.
3. Canada is the largest provider of food for the United Nations.

Welcome to Warbrides, *Wartime Information Board booklet, Department of National Defence, 1944.*

Here Comes the Bride

The *Aquitania* arrived Tuesday evening and we watched the ship come in. The band played "O Canada" and "Here Comes the Bride," and the wives threw down English coins to those on the dock like us, and everyone was happy, despite the drizzle.

Wednesday noon, I left with the first train of four. Each was ten cars long, filled with brides — two trains for the west, two trains for Toronto and Montreal. There were three army officers, one medical officer, one WD officer (Women's Division, RCAF) and varying numbers of Red Cross volunteers, never more than four, on board each train — so you see, Pop, I didn't do it all myself.

We had a fairly easy trip across Canada, as these trips go. The worst is getting up at all hours to dump people into the arms of waiting husbands. I could almost write an essay on styles and ways of greeting long separated husbands and wives. Our worst worry was that whenever we stopped, 20 minutes or more at some small town, they would rush out to buy things — fruit, clothes, shoes, anything. Some of them went completely berserk, because they didn't need coupons and it was pathetic the things they bought and the prices they paid. Naturally, they weren't used to handling Canadian money, and unfortunately all our shopkeepers weren't the honest type.

Also, there was too much country for them. They got bored with trees, then lakes, then prairies. Just too much of them, they said. *Excerpt from a letter by a Women's Division, RCAF officer, dated May 6, 1946.*

A Rough Sea Journey

It was the end of the world for my parents when I came to Canada. They thought they would never see me again. Every time a brown paper envelope arrived for me from Sackville House, from the immigration people, my father started to rant and rave, and my mother would cry.

Eventually, a letter came, saying I must report to Crewe, to the ladies' waiting room at the railway station, and no one was to know about it — the war was still on then. But my father said, "To hell with that," so I was the only one who came with a father. Two Canadian officers were standing at the door, barring the way. They asked to see my identification papers, and my father demanded to see theirs. What a start to the journey!

We sailed from Liverpool, on the *Louis Pasteur*, with ninety-nine warbrides on board, only one with a child. The other passengers were returning troops, mostly wounded men. We slept in huge cabins, in three-tier bunks, with two guards at the end of the passageway to see that no men came in. But they needn't have worried about me. At eleven o'clock, the steward helped me into my bunk, and I was so sick, I stayed there till we docked at Halifax. They brought huge drums for us to be sick into.

They took the wounded men off first, on stretchers, and an hour later our names were called. As we went down the gang plank, an air-man took each of us by the arm, down to the immigration shed and then to the railway station counter, where you could choose fruit, candy, a book — anything you wanted. Then he put you onto the train.

GLOSSARY	
ENGLISH	CANADIAN
Motorcar	Automobile
Multiple shops	Chain Stores
Parafin	Coal oil
Pavement	Sidewalk
Petrol	Gasoline
Plate	Silverware
Plum cake	Fruit cake
Pillar box	Mail box
Post (of a letter)	Mail
Reel of cotton	Spool of thread
Rubber	Eraser
Scent	Perfume
Shopwalker	Floorwalker
Silencer (motor-car)	Muffler
Sledge	Sled
Snowboots	Overshoes or Galoshes
Spanner	Wrench
Spirits	Liquor
Stalls	Orchestra seats
Steadings	Farm buildings
Suspenders	Garters
Sweets	Candy
Sweet or pudding	Dessert
Tart	Pie
Teats	Nipples
Tin	Can
Torch	Flashlight

Welcome to Warbrides, *Wartime Information Board booklet, Department of National Defence, 1944.*

Some brides complained — they said they were treated like children, but I thought they did a wonderful job. The first meal on the train was breakfast, and they served me six slices of bacon and two eggs. Imagine, two eggs and all that bacon! I ate everything they put in front of me. *Welsh warbride, 1944.*

"Food made such an impression . . . . "

The food which didn't get eaten in the dining hall was thrown overboard every day, and I would stand at the rail, watching it float away behind us. "What an awful waste," I thought. We'd been so short of food in England, we never wasted anything, not a scrap.

Food made such an impression on me, when I first arrived. People would talk about how difficult it was to get butter here, and I'd think of my mother, going out with her ration book, and queuing up, and coming home frozen, and saying, "How marvellous! I got a little bit of fish."

There was a terrific spirit in England in the war, but people here didn't seem to understand what the war was about. It seemed a very long way away. They didn't ask Roy very much about what he'd done, and yet he'd been overseas for five years. *English warbride.*

"The farmer's wife . . . . "

The farmer's wife must know how to handle a wood-burning stove. Except where coalfields are near, wood is used almost entirely in farm homes, for both heating and cooking. In the prairie provinces, about one farm in four uses coal for heating and cooking. In Ontario, some coal is used for heating, and about one farm in seven has gas or electricity for cooking. In Quebec, a small percentage of farmers' wives cook with gas or electricity.

Though usually comfortable, a Canadian farm home is not luxurious. You have only one chance in five of having electric light in a farm home, which means you must use coal oil (paraffin) lamps. You have only eight chances in a hundred of finding any sort of plumbing in a farm home, outside facilities taking its place. Six farm homes out of ten have radios (wireless), three have telephones, and nearly half have motor cars. One third of Canada's farm homes have none of these conveniences. A considerable number are in need of repairs.

This is not said to discourage you, but to give you a real picture of farm life in Canada. It is not an easy life, but if you've got the stuff to make a farmer's wife, it is one of the most satisfying existences imaginable.

Welcome to Warbrides, *Wartime Information Board booklet, Department of National Defence, 1944.*

A Happy Surprise

Soon after I arrived in Fort Erie, I was invited round to this neighbour's house. I was standing in the hallway, talking to her, when suddenly, all the doors opened, and people bounded out, saying, "Surprise! Surprise!" I was surprised alright, and I thought, "So what?" I'd never heard of a shower.

We all went into the living room, and we played parlour games. Then somebody brought in a child's wagon decorated like a ship, and it was full of gifts. I just ignored it, because I was embarrassed. I thought I was supposed to put something in it, and I hadn't brought anything with me. After a while, someone said, "Aren't you going to open your presents?" There were so many handmade things, a crocheted lace table cloth, embroidered pillow slips and towels. I was so full of emotion, I started to cry. *Welsh warbride.*

YWCA Christmas party for warbrides, Calgary, 1946.

The Honeymoon

His birthday was the day after we were married, and I didn't even know. That's how little I knew about him. I was seventeen, and I met him at church, just before VE Day. He was an orderly in the medical corps, and he was twenty-seven. I saw him every evening for a couple of months, before he went to Europe; and we'd walk in the park for a couple of hours, until my mother called me in at ten o'clock.

I spent the whole trip wondering how he'd be. And when he met me in Winnipeg, off the train, I didn't even recognize him — I'd never seen him out of uniform. He was a different man from the one who courted me, and we were very strange with each other, at first.

We went to a hotel room he'd taken, and I saw this pile of cigarette butts in the ashtray by the bed. Then I realised he was as nervous as I was. I had a lot of growing up to do. *English warbride, 1946.*

Dutch warbrides arrive at Bonaventure Station, Montreal, November 1946. Returning troops had first claim on available shipping immediately after the war, and warbrides had the next priority. Wives and children of Canadian servicemen were brought to Canada free of charge, most of them in military transports.

III   DP meant Displaced Persons

IN 1947, WHEN THE INTERNATIONAL Refugee Organization (IRO) was set up by the United Nations, there were more than one million displaced persons in Europe. From German-occupied countries, these people had been sent to Germany to work as labourers in the mines and factories and on the land. After the war, they either could not return to their country of origin, or they refused to go back after a Communist government took power. The largest numbers were Poles, Ukrainians, Jews, Yugoslavs, Estonians, Latvians and Lithuanians. In the postwar years, these homeless people were joined by political refugees who fled their homelands, rather than live under the new Communist regimes in eastern Europe.

1947 was the year Mackenzie King, under pressure from Canadian employers and ethnic groups, announced his government's decision to admit refugees to help ease the acute labour shortage. In the twelve months beginning in April 1947, 20,000 were admitted to Canada, either through the ''close relatives'' scheme, or as part of the sponsored labour movement, which brought refugees here on one-year labour contracts. They were mainly employed in agriculture, lumbering, railway maintenance, mining, heavy construction, iron manufacturing, textiles and domestic service.

Ethnic German refugees, known as *Volksdeutsch*, did not come under the mandate of the IRO, because of their origin. But many were brought to Canada by the Canadian Christian Council for the Resettlement of Refugees. Members included the Canadian Mennonite Board of Colonization, the Canadian Lutheran World Relief, the German Baptist Union, and the Catholic Immigrant Aid Society.

Forty families shared this stove, located in a passageway, in this refugee camp in Germany.

Under the government's sponsored labour scheme, these people were admitted to Canada under one-year contracts to work on farms or railways, or in particular industries. Sometimes, the scheme worked satisfactorily for all parties. Sometimes, workers left before their year was up, causing complaints from disappointed employers. Sometimes, workers were exploited and mistreated, and, occasionally, stories about them appeared in the press.

In 1948, an account of "misery and squalor" in a displaced persons' camp for sugar beet workers in Emerson, Manitoba was published in newspapers across Canada. The Winnipeg *Tribune*, where the story first appeared, described the primitive accommodation where workers lived, twenty to a hut, with one galvanized iron sink which served as washstand, bath tub and clothes washer. The men complained about mice chewing holes in coats and blankets, and about "bad pork" which had given thirty-nine of the sixty-five workers diarrhea. "The most disgusting feature of the whole business is the fact that the men who complained were apparently kept in line by threats of deportation," said the Edmonton *Journal*, recalling the evils of indentured labour schemes earlier in the century, and the inadequate supervision of the present program. "We don't want a class of semi-serfs growing up in Canada, even temporarily."

The Manitoba sugar beet workers were brought to Canada through the Department of Labour, and an official investigation was launched immediately. Other workers were hired directly by private employers, and one of these gained considerable notoriety in 1947. Ludger Dionne, who also happened to be the Liberal member of parliament for St. Georges de Beauce, imported five hundred girls from European refugee camps to work in the Dionne Spinning Mills, and, to avoid the delays caused by the shipping shortage, he arranged for them to be flown to Canada. But, as the press discovered, the workers were obliged to repay their $300 airfare out of an extremely meager salary. Their two-year contracts specified that they would start work at 25¢ an hour, or $12 for a forty-eight-hour week. Out of that $12, $3 was deducted to pay for their airfare, and a further $6 for room and board at the neighbouring convent run by the Sisters of the Good Shepherd. That left the workers with $3 a week spending money, and an "understanding" that they would not marry, or leave, until the cost of their airfare had been repaid. Dionne protested about his humanitarian motives in finding work for such a large number of refugees, and bringing them so quickly to Canada, but the press, and various of his fellow MPs, reacted skeptically.

Canada's preference, shared by the United States and Australia, for those displaced persons young enough and strong enough to do physical labour provoked complaints from both inside and outside the country. The IRO complained about the large numbers rejected as too old or too frail. When the IRO sought to persuade receiving countries to accept some sick refugees needing institutional care, ten thousand cases were resettled, but Canada accepted so few, she was not listed among those countries taking two hundred or more. Concern was also expressed about the fate of the so-called "forgotten elite": the hard core of 40,000 former professionals, including doctors, lawyers, engineers and university professors, who were not employable as farmers, foresters, miners or construction workers.

Sometimes, brawn and brains happened to go hand in hand, but when they did, educational qualifications and professional skills often had to be hidden from Canadian immigration teams recruiting labour in European refugee camps. In 1949, the same year that the IRO drew attention to Europe's "forgotten elite," the Canadian Jewish Congress presented a brief to the Canadian government, calling for the "lifting of what has

Displaced Person, Emerson, Manitoba farm workers' camp, 1948.

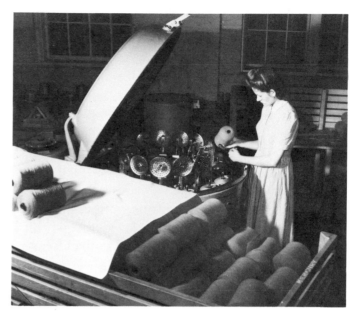

Displaced Person working at Dionne Spinning Mills, St. Georges, Beauce County, Quebec, 1948.

become known as a virtual exclusion of brains."

The IRO recommended that Canada admit a thousand professionals, under sponsorship by voluntary agencies and service clubs, but while the Immigration Branch did prepare a Cabinet document suggesting a possible quota of five hundred, no formal target was ever set. In 1949, the Ottawa *Citizen* had claimed that the policy of barring highly qualified people was based on pressure from professional associations and particularly

from doctors and teachers. This claim was seemingly substantiated by the way the Immigration Branch was rebuffed when it approached various professional groups.

The Canadian Medical Association said that European graduates since 1935 were reported to be of low standard and unable to meet Canadian and United States standards. The Canadian Dental Association said European standards were "unacceptable," and that it was impossible to provide training to bring Europeans up to Canadian standards. The Forest Engineers said very few Europeans could meet their requirements; the Engineering Institute said there was "no demand" for engineers; and the Ontario Schoolteachers suggested that the only way European refugee teachers could be absorbed was as clerical workers. Only the Canadian Nurses Association responded positively, reporting a shortage of nurses, and volunteering the information that, in some provinces, nurses could work for one year as a nurse's aide, and then write the provincial examination.

European physicians who succeeded in entering Canada shortly after the war generally found their reception by the medical establishment to be an embittering experience. One Estonian refugee eventually returned to Europe, after the New Brunswick Medical Council refused to give him permission to write the Dominion Medical Examinations. Johannes Riives had been a professor of neuro-surgery in Estonia, and was considered "the best neuro-surgeon in the Maritime provinces" by the Superintendent of the Provincial Medical Hospital in Fairville, New Brunswick — a recommendation which did not affect the Council's decision. A similar situation existed in Alberta, where, in 1950-51, it was alleged that the provincial government had threatened to take over the licensing of doctors from the medical association, in order to break a virtual closed shop.

After 1950, however, attitudes began to change. Over two hundred of Europe's "forgotten elite" were eventually sponsored by Canadian service organizations, and professional associations began to open their doors, even if only part-way. Hungarian architects, Polish engineers, Czech doctors, Lithuanian dentists and Latvian teachers began to gain entry to their professions in Canada. These advances marked the beginning of Canadian recognition that central and eastern Europeans were not just the hewers of wood and drawers of water that they had been considered since the turn of the century.

Displaced Persons, Union Station, Toronto.

In November 1946, the first of 4,500 Polish war veterans arrived at Halifax aboard the *SS Sea Robin*. They came to Canada as agricultural workers, with two-year contracts, and were brought in to replace German prisoners of war who had just been sent back to Europe. All the Poles were members of the Second Polish Army Corps, which had fought in Italy as part of the British Eighth Army, and all had refused repatriation to Poland, now under Communist rule.

Polish refugees en route to Hamilton, Ontario, 1948.

Bring Workers into Canada to Replace Nazis

Headline in Ottawa *Citizen*, May 30, 1946, after Agriculture Minister James Gardiner told the House of Commons that 4,000 prisoners of war working on Canadian farms would be sent back to Europe, and an unspecified group of workers imported to replace them.

"What a welcome for war heroes . . . ."

Our group came on a ship from Naples, in November 1946. When we landed in Halifax, we were given work clothes to wear on the farm, and these clothes had numbers on them. We discovered they had been worn by German prisoners of war. They left them behind when they went back to Europe.

What a welcome for war heroes, because that's what we thought we were. *Polish war veteran.*

"A moral obligation"

The resettlement of refugees and displaced persons constitutes a special problem. Canada is not obliged, as a result of membership in the United Nations, or under the constitution of the International Refugee Organization, to accept any specific number of refugees or displaced persons. We have, nevertheless, a moral obligation to assist in meeting the problem.

The government is sending immigration officers to examine the situation among the refugee groups, and to take steps towards the early admission of some thousands of their number.

Prime Minister Mackenzie King, speaking in the House of Commons, May 1, 1947.

"Hard-boiled officials . . . ."

Efforts will undoubtedly be made by those in the Polish Forces who see an opportunity to get to Canada, but who, once they come here, will be looking for "white collar jobs," and it will require some hard-boiled officials to prevent these gentlemen from being included in the category of "agricultural workers." Our officers are continually confronted with this problem overseas.

A. L. Jolliffe, Director of Immigration, to Dr. A. MacNamara, Deputy Minister of Labour, August 1, 1946.

Effect on Polish Morale

United Kingdom recognises that our present willingness to take Polish personnel is linked with our loss of prisoner of war labour, but urges that this relationship not be unduly stressed in any publicity given these arrangements because of adverse effect it would have on Polish morale.

Telegram from the High Commissioner for Canada in Great Britain to the Under-Secretary of State for External Affairs, Ottawa, June 5, 1946.

Tragic Failure

Over 6,000,000 Jewish civilians have died violently and unnecessarily as the result of the preachings of Hitler and of the latent spirit of anti-Semitism which permeates the continent of Europe. It is my duty to say that the number of these victims could have been very much smaller and very many of their lives could have been saved, if such countries as Canada would have paid due heed to the requests and pleas of their kin, and of Jewish citizens, to grant a refuge to some of them while there was still time.

It is a simple and truthful fact that because the applications made to the Immigration Branch on behalf of many of them were not favourably acted upon, their ashes and bones today lie in Buchenwald, and soap has been made of their bodies, instead of their being free and useful citizens in Canada today.

Saul Hayes, National Executive Director, Canadian Jewish Congress, appearing before the Senate Standing Committee on Immigration and Labour, 1946.

Ted Kramolc drawing, 1946: *Letter*.

(The Senate Committee was told that, between 1933 and 1944, Canada admitted nearly 18,000 European refugees, and a further 3,000 on temporary entry permits. About 7,000 of these refugees were Jewish. The United States, by comparison, took in 250,000, more than half of them Jewish. — Author)

"Living conditions are deplorable."

I found 1,338 people living in the camp, awaiting transportation to Canada. Accommodation is only adequate for 550, and living conditions are deplorable.

Very few beds have mattresses. Some have paliasses filled with straw, but in the majority of cases, the people are sleeping on loose straw. I did not see any tables or chairs.

I was informed that last June the camp was fumigated and disinfected, but vermin again became prevalent and on the 10th inst. they had to disinfect the camp again. The chemical used in this disinfestation was so strong that it killed all the gardens under cultivation between the different buildings. There is no running water in any of the buildings, and the washing and toilet facilities are provided for in central washrooms, one for men and one for women. For washing purposes, there are long troughs equipped with cold water faucets approximately every two feet. These washrooms are used for personal bathing, laundry and the preparation of vegetables for table use. Portions of the same building contain lavatory facilities but there was no running water, and I found that latrine buckets were emptied daily.

In the huts used for sleeping quarters, countless windows required glazing and were stuffed with old rags and cardboard. I noticed 12 people billeted in one room, measuring 15' by 24', which had only one small window for ventilation, and in one Neisen hut there were 16 beds with no light or ventilation other than the door.

P. W. Bird of the Canadian Immigration Mission, reporting on conditions in the Muehlenberg refugee camp in the British zone, Germany, August 23, 1948.

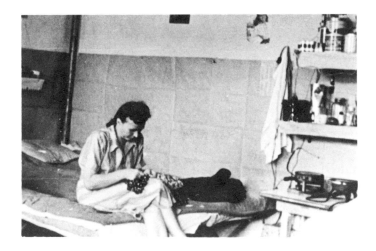

Ludwigsburg camp, Germany. Canadian immigration teams operated in Germany and Austria, from March 1947, selecting would-be immigrants from the refugee camps. Teams consisted of an immigration inspector, a medical officer, a security officer and a Labour Department representative.

Mennonite children in refugee camp, Germany. Ethnic German refugees, known as *Volksdeutsch*, did not come under the mandate of the International Refugee Organization. Many were brought to Canada by the Canadian Christian Council for the Resettlement of Refugees.

"Canada took me . . . ."

My camp was in the British occupation zone, and there was so little food to begin with — just turnips and potatoes and thin soup. One loaf of bread was cut into fourteen slices, and one piece was a whole day's bread ration for each person. Black "coffee" was actually roasted peas and beans.

Beds were made of straw, and only sick people got pillows. There were no sheets — we slept under army blankets. We had no cigarettes. The soldiers had lots, but they weren't supposed to give them to us. But some soldiers would light a cigarette, take a puff and throw it away. Then we'd pick it up so quick.

By 1947, things were much better. Sometimes we got stew, and that was terrific, and there was

white bread on Sundays. We had a high school in the camp, we even had a good soccer team. But the depressing thing was that there was no future there, and I was in that camp for three and a half years. The future would only begin when some country took us away from there. And Canada took me away, in 1949. *Yugoslav refugee.*

Fooled the Doctor

A poster went up in our camp, saying that Canada was looking for lumberjacks. To qualify, you had to be single, and you had to pass a medical test to see if you were strong enough for the work. The doctor always looked at your hands, to see if you had done manual labour before.

Every afternoon for two weeks before the medical, several of us volunteered to chop wood for the camp kitchen, to get callouses on our hands. I don't know if I really fooled the doctor, and I was a big man anyway. But I was so happy I passed the test. I'd been in that camp for two and a half years. *Slovenian refugee.*

Medical Inspection

We were screened for physical fitness, and it was not a very private affair. First we were checked for fleas and lice, in a detoxication centre. I saw some official put a duster gun, a flea powder dispenser, up my fifteen-year-old sister's skirt, and down her blouse.

Later, they separated the sexes for the medical inspection, and I'm not sure what happened to my mother and my sister. But for the men, this check wasn't very private either. My father and I stood stark naked in line with many other men, waiting our turn. Fortunately, all they found wrong with me was my "lazy eye." *Volksdeutsch, 1949.*

Canada: Jobs for You. The Land of Tomorrow said a Department of Labour poster displayed in European refugee camps.

Working conditions

The current rate of wages paid in this area for general labour is $6.20 per day, from which $1.20 is deducted for board and lodging. The work done at these camps consists mainly of felling timber, cutting it into lengths, piling and hauling the logs.

Department of Labour information for workers accepting employment in Northern Ontario, 1947.

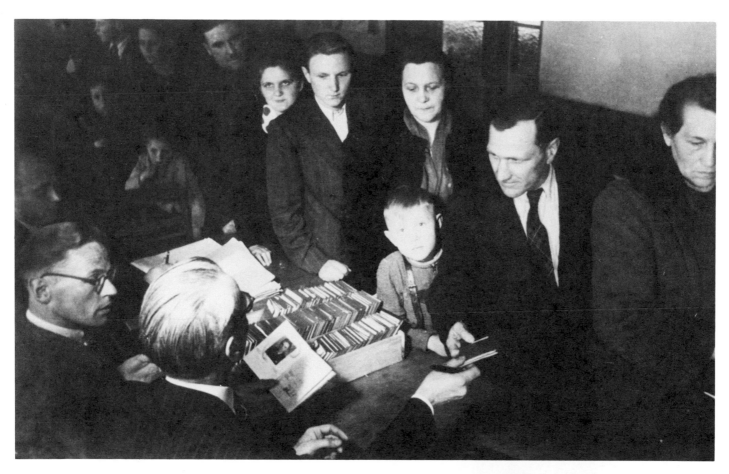

Ethnic German refugees from eastern Europe
exchange German identity cards for travel documents
to Canada.

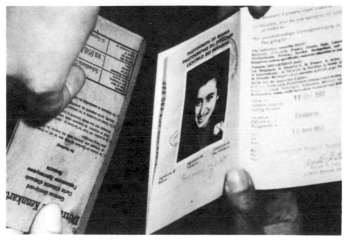

"The part that hurt . . . ."

The hardest hit were the professionals, because nobody wanted us — the doctors, the lawyers, the accountants, the school teachers. And yet, there were so many of us in the camps.

If you were young and healthy, you might get hired as a labourer or a domestic, as long as you hid your qualifications. That was the part that hurt, having to lie about your status. I was a dentist in Lithuania, but I came as a domestic, and even domestics had their muscles examined, just like slaves.

Yet we were the lucky ones. Many, many people weren't accepted because they weren't healthy, or they were too old for hard work. *Lithuanian refugee.*

Selection of Domestic Workers

Apparently, many girls we are passing fail to disclose the fact that they have higher education. While it is agreed that we will pass up to 10% who disclose having superior education, wherever it is suspected that any girls possess such qualifications, but are concealing them, please reject.

As a general average minimum, at least about 15% of those presented should be rejected . . . .

Department of Labour directive to the Canadian Government Immigration Mission employees, February 1948.

Doctors Needed Elsewhere

Let it not be said that the Canadian Medical Association is uncharitable or unkindly in its thinking towards these professional brethren who find themselves in such a sorry plight. But it is incomprehensible to me that the Government of Canada will so disregard its international obligations that refugee physicians will be admitted to Canada, when all indications point to the wisdom of settling them in the needy areas of the globe. It must, therefore, be a very narrow humanitarian viewpoint which will suggest that refugee physicians should be brought to Canada when their services are so urgently needed elsewhere.

A. D. Kelly, Assistant Secretary to the Canadian Medical Association, in a September 1947 submission to the Immigration Branch.

Ukrainian family, en route to British Columbia.

Volksdeutsch refugees aboard the *S.S. Beaverbrae*, arriving at Halifax. This ship left Bremerhaven for Halifax every thirty-five days in 1948, with 773 refugees on board. The *Beaverbrae* was formerly the *Huascaran*, of the Hamburg-Amerika Line, and the 7,000 ton diesel-electric liner had been used by the Germans as a submarine repair depot during the war. She was awarded to Canada under reparation settlements, purchased by Canadian Pacific, and made available to the Canadian Christian Council for Refugees in 1948, for sending refugees to Canada.

The Beaverbrae

Provisions placed on board in Canadian ports for 773 passengers and 116 crew on each voyage include: potatoes, 10 tons; fresh meat, 8 tons; and smoked meat, 3 tons; flour, 7 tons; fresh vegetables, 4 tons; butter and cheese, 2 tons; strained baby foods, 300 tins; eggs, 20,000; poultry, 4 tons.

For the benefit of sugar-starved European passengers, the *Beaverbrae's* stores will include 2 tons of sugar proper, plus 1 ton of jams and marmalade, 16,000 chocolate bars and 36,000 bags of hard candy. *Canadian Pacific press release, 1948.*

A Film about Canada

They showed us a film on board ship about life in Canada, but it was really about the 1930s. I'll never forget one scene out west, where this poor fellow was building a house, and a terrific wind blew the walls down. It made us wonder what in the world would happen to us in Palmer, Saskatchewan. *Volksdeutsch, 1950.*

Refugees in dining hall on board the *General M. L. Hersey.*

Bring in Families

I said to my people, "When these simple souls come from Germany and Austria, remember, it is important to see that their first impression of this country is a good one. These poor people have not had much to eat in Europe. Have some hostels ready, and see that these people are given a good meal. Give them a steak, first of all, when they get here. That kind of thing pays dividends; they never forget it.

I am of the opinion that the best people you can bring into a country are families. I was a member of a large family myself, and with a large family, you get stability. You get a number of children and their father and mother. That is the stuff that empires are built out of.

Humphrey Mitchell, Minister of Labour, appearing before the Senate Standing Committee on Immigration and Labour, March 22, 1949.

"To die in the open air."

There were about eighty people altogether in each huge dormitory. Men and boys slept in one place, and women and girls in another. Kids up to nine years old had to go with their mothers. Boy, did it ever stink down there, with all the puking. My wife told me she was going to die. I said, "You come on up above, on deck. It's better to die in the open air."

To pack in as many people as possible on that ship, there was only a skeleton crew on board, and they called for volunteers to help feed the passengers and keep the ship clean. I worked in the butcher's shop, cutting up meat, from early morning till late at night. When we left the ship, the crew gave me a suitcase full of food — bread and sausage, apples and cheese. After two and a half days on the train, we still had some left. *Volksdeutsch, 1949.*

I.D. Tags

In the camp, we were each given a ticket which we wore in our lapels. It had your name, your number, the name of the boat and the date you were to leave. The Jewish children on our ship wore their tickets around their necks, on string with a lead seal.

Once we got to Canada, we got another ticket to wear, and this one showed our destination. *Serbian refugee, 1948.*

Displaced Persons arrive at Halifax, July 1947, on board the US military transport *General M.B. Stewart*, one of a fleet of 36 ships chartered by the International Refugee Organization, a United Nations' agency.

Tattoo Marks

One problem group of Displaced Persons came forward in September 1947, by the *S.S. General M. B. Stewart*, in the bulk movement of lumber workers. While the vessel was on the sea, we received a cable from our representative in Germany (Mr. Cormier) stating that about 25 of these Displaced Persons were suspected to have been former German Storm Troopers. This suspicion arose at the time of embarkation, when it was too late to stop them.

When the vessel arrived at Halifax, these men were all very carefully checked by the RCMP and our Inspector-in-Charge, with the assistance of the IRO escorting officer. The suspicion had been based on the fact that these men had tattoo marks on their bodies, which might have indicated membership in the German forces. However, upon very careful and thorough examination and questioning, the conclusion was reached that the tattoo marks had been made while they were in German concentration and labour camps and did not indicate any connection with the SS or other undesirable German organizations. Finally the whole group was cleared and allowed to proceed.

I. R. Stirling, Assistant Commissioner of Immigration, reporting to the Minister of Citizenship and Immigration in October 1950, following claims by the Canadian Jewish Congress that former Nazis were entering Canada as refugees.

Immigrant family in detention quarters, Halifax, April 1951. New arrivals could be refused admission for health reasons, including active tuberculosis, trachoma and venereal disease. Mental illness was another ground for rejection. But the actual number of people turned back from Canadian ports was small (between 20 and 50 a year in this period) because would-be

"Behind bars again."

These cousins who sponsored us sent us the fare to Winnipeg, but they made a mistake. When we landed, we had not enough money for our train tickets. The Immigration officers kept us there, in a room with bars on the windows for six days, waiting for the money to come.

We asked, could we have permission to visit Halifax while we waited? No, not until the money came, and then we could see the city. It was very strange. We said to ourselves, "We have come to a free country, and here we are behind bars again."

This word "DP" was a terrible thing. Our cousins' daughter told us, when we got to Winnipeg, "We don't want any DPs here." She was fourteen years old. We were treated as if we came on their mercy. They expected us to look poor. Well, we were poor alright, but we didn't *look* poor. I'm a tailor, and we dressed top notch.

Former immigrants were the toughest, particularly the ones who came in the 1920s. They had a hard time in the Depression, and they resented us coming, when things were starting to get better. They said, "Canada is giving you everything on a plate, you dirty DPs."

We had to prove to them that we were human, like themselves, that we were proud, that we could be entrepreneurs too. *Polish immigrant, Winnipeg.*

immigrants were screened first in Europe. About 350 a year, however, were turned back or later deported for "civil" reasons, which included security as well as criminality. Proven Nazi, Fascist, or Communist adherents were not admissible.

Estonians arriving at St. John, New Brunswick, aboard an 80-foot sailboat, August 1948, after a 61-day, 6,000 mile voyage from Sweden. During the next two years, over 1,000 Baltic refugees reached Canada in small, crowded, ill-equipped vessels. Although they came illegally, only twelve were ordered to return to Sweden as "undesirables."

The Boat People

We were so scared when the Swedish government gave up our Latvian officers to the Russians. We felt we had to get away, far away, in case the Russians got us too.

Two hundred and fifty of us Latvians and Estonians living in Sweden got together and put up some money. Five of us went to Britain to put down a deposit on an old, war-surplus minesweeper, the *Sarabande*, and we sailed her back to Sweden and fixed her up. Many of us were professional sailors. I'd been an engineer in the merchant marine, so I was made Chief Engineer, and my father, who was a retired sea captain, was the mate. The captain was Estonian.

We thought we'd try Canada first, but if Canada wouldn't have us, we would sail down the coast to the United States, and then, if necessary, to South America. Someone would take us in, we thought.

If you don't have a flag, you're a pirate ship, and that's what we were. No one would let us fly their flag — Sweden, Panama, Nicaragua, they all refused — so we voted in a democratic way on which flag it should be: Latvian or Estonian? There were more Latvians than Estonians, so we hoisted the Latvian flag.

We had to keep away from regular shipping lanes, so we took a far northerly route, which brought us at last to Newfoundland. Our ship was old and small and very slow, and it took almost four weeks, after we stopped in Cork to take on bunker coal. There were 258 men, women and children on board, and we lived off Icelandic herring and potatoes all the time we were at sea.

In Halifax, when we arrived, they put most of

Baltic refugees on board the converted **minesweeper** *Walnut*, which reached Halifax in December 1948. 347 Baltic refugees reached Sydney, Nova Scotia in December 1948, jammed into a former minesweeper built to accommodate a 14-man crew. The voyage from Sweden aboard the *Walnut* took 28 days.

In November 1949, Canadian immigration authorities arranged to examine refugees on board one ship in Cork, southern Ireland, where it had stopped for fuel "to prevent the hardship and risk involved in 372 souls crossing the Atlantic at this time of year in a small vessel, not properly filled with life-saving equipment. **Air transport was provided for this group.**"

Sarabande passengers in detention, Halifax, August 1949.

us in a camp, while they decided whether we could stay. They had to find out if we were criminals, or sick people. We were there for two and a half months. But fifteen of us sailors, the ship's crew, stayed on board, and kept the ship ready to go. Argentina was the country we thought we would try next.

But, at last, they told us we were accepted, and we were asked where we would like to go. Did we have relatives in Canada? I had an uncle and aunt in British Columbia, and they got a farmer there to say he'd employ us. The Canadian government paid for our train fares and our meals, and we never had to repay the money. *Latvian refugee, 1949.*

(*The Captain of the* Sarabande *was taken to court, and fined a token $100, which the Lutheran Church paid on his behalf. The ship itself was confiscated. — Author*)

"The best advertisement . . . ."

The bulk of the refugees consist of the better class of people. I have been forced to admire their determination, thriftiness and adaptability. In my opinion Canada will never be sorry for taking Baltic people as every last one of them are the best advertisement we will get in our country against Communism. *I. A. Ewen, Immigration Officer-in-Charge, Sweden, reporting to Ottawa, May 16, 1949.*

"A free man now . . . ."

It took two and a half or three days to get from Quebec City to Regina. Your heart beats a little faster, you know, the closer you get, and I thought to myself, "Who is going to be out there to meet me? There's got to be *somebody* there to tell me what to do." The conductor on the train says, "This is your destination, this is where you get off." So I get off, and there are all sorts of people in the railway station, but nobody looks at me. So that's it. I am on my own, a free man now, in a free country. *Ukrainian refugee.*

"You look crazy too."

I came in the winter. When I got off the train in Hamilton, I had no stockings, and open-toed shoes, but I was wearing my fur coat. I had slept under it as a blanket all through the war. There were some women on the platform laughing and pointing at me. They didn't know that I understood English. I went up to them and I said, "You go through war in Europe, you look crazy too." *Polish refugee, Ontario.*

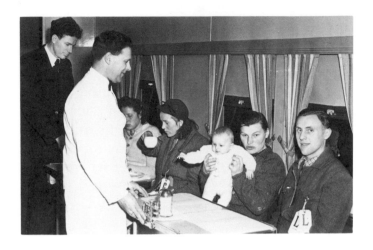

"So much empty space."

We took the train to Winnipeg, and I thought that wilderness would never end. So much bush, so much empty space. Europe is so densely populated, and here there were no people, it seemed, for hundreds of miles. But then we came to Winnipeg, a big railway station, a big city with lots of people. And our relatives waiting for us, to take us home. Mother hadn't seen her sister for more than twenty years. *Russian Mennonite, Manitoba.*

On Christmas Eve . . .

My first Christmas was at the station. The train arrived in Vancouver on Christmas Eve, and there was a big Christmas tree with beautiful decorations, and "Silent Night" playing over the loudspeaker. I sat there for a long time, looking at the lights and listening to the music. Then the Traveller's Aid lady called the Y, and they found me a room for $2. *Polish refugee, British Columbia.*

Refugees Keen for New Life, Want to Jitterbug, Hear Bing

Ten vivacious girls from displaced persons camps in Germany hadn't mastered the English way of saying "Canada is good," but there was no mistaking their unanimous opinion as they arrived at the CPR station at 9:30 a.m. Tuesday to work and make their homes at the Keith Sanatorium.

When an *Albertan* reporter boarded their train at Gleichen, 51 miles east of Calgary, at 8:00 a.m., the ten bright-eyed girls were up and already chattering merrily in six languages about their new home.

As the train rolled westward, conversation resembled a game of "Twenty Questions." Several girls spoke some German, and all shouted encouragement at the reporter as she tried to follow them with the help of a Polish-English glossary and a German grammar book.

The first common ground was found when "Do you smoke?" was found in the glossary by Luba, a dark-haired native of Kiev. Then Janina, a dark-eyed, smiling Polish girl triumphantly shouted, "Players, Please!" Luba produced a package of Old Golds, which she offered with a smiling "Amerikanisch."

Regina became enthusiastic at the mention of movies, and all the girls nodded their heads vigorously at the mention of Clark Gable, although Bing Crosby was the star who really brought forth smiles. At the mention of Frank Sinatra, Regina put her head on one side and adopted a soulful expression which would be recognized anywhere as belonging to "the voice."

When questioned as to how they liked Canadians, the girls were all enthusiastic. Again, faced

Polish Displaced Persons employed at a Calgary
sanatorium.

Too much Publicity

with language difficulties, Luba and Anna demonstrated the difference between a German fraulein and a Canadian girl on a train. "Here is the German," said Luba, and she turned and stared out the window, ignoring Anna, her travelling companion. "But the Canadian —" she turned and beamed at Anna, and the two engaged in a lively conversation in Polish. "So you see, the Canadians, they talk, they're friendly." Calgary Albertan, *October 15, 1947.*

Disturbance was expressed regarding the glamour publicity being given in the newspapers, and the Chairman was asked whether the Department officially could take steps to correct the false impression now held by the public. The Chairman did not feel the matter was serious enough to warrant official protest to the press.

Minutes of the meeting of the Committee of Reception and Placement, Department of Labour, November 6, 1947.

Ukrainian and Polish orphans, Mount Mary Immaculate Orphanage, Ancaster, Ontario, run by the Sisters Servants of Mary Immaculate. In 1948, 1,000 Catholic war orphans, mostly Polish and Ukrainian, were admitted to Canada under a special Order-in-Council, as well as 1,000 Jewish war orphans, a number which was eventually increased to 1,200.

"Love and Concern"

When I was asked whether I wanted to go to Vancouver or Montreal, or Toronto, or Halifax, I asked for a map of Canada. I saw that Winnipeg was in the middle of the continent and I said, "That's where I want to go, it looks safe."

The family I was based with mended me. They really put me together and they did it with the only glue that can put human beings together. They did it with love and concern. *Hungarian Jewish war orphan.*

Faith Rekindled

My first family didn't believe that I was Jewish. A Jewish child after the war who doesn't *speak* Jewish? Doesn't *look* Jewish? Because I didn't. I'd been hidden by a Czech family, they pretended I was their niece. But on Friday, this woman lit the candles, and I said, "I haven't seen Shabbat candles in I don't know how long," and she said, "Maybe you are Jewish, after all." *Czech Jewish war orphan.*

Jewish War orphans,
West Germany, 1945.

Selection of Orphan Children

In selecting orphan children for placement and adoption in Canada, one of the most important factors is the social background of the family. A bad background means the possibility of accepting an unmanageable and incorrigible child. The acceptance of illegitimate children materially increases the risk.

A. L. Jolliffe, Director of Immigration, to Dr. Hugh Keenleyside, Deputy Minister of Mines and Resources, in March 1949, after receiving a report from Karlsruhe, Germany, that some Catholic orphans being presented to Immigration officials were illegitimate.

Official Reply

There is nothing in the experience of child care agencies to suggest that illegitimate children, as such, are a greater risk than others. The important factor, of course, is the kind of treatment the child has received up to the point of adoption.

Dr. Hugh Keenleyside to A. L. Jolliffe, after consultation with the Executive Director of the Canadian Welfare Council, March 1949.

Clothing collected for Jewish refugees arriving from Europe, Montreal, late 1940s.

"Bread is very important to me . . . ."

Just before the train left Halifax, I ran into the store in the station and bought a loaf of white bread. "Look at the wonderful white bread you can get for 12¢!" I said.

Bread is very important to me, and I can never throw away a piece of bread. I lost my entire family in Auschwitz — my parents, my sisters, my brothers, my aunts and uncles and their families, fifty-one people in all. During those years, I had a fantasy which I think helped me to keep my sanity, to stay alive. I kept thinking that, one day, someone would put in front of me a large loaf of bread, on a plate, and I could eat it all. Just bread, you understand, nothing else. *Polish Jew.*

"To work on the farms."

It was a sort of accident that I came to Saskatchewan. I escaped from Czechoslovakia in 1950, and went to Germany. I was a house painter, and I wanted to go to Australia, but they were only taking a certain number. Canada was still open, and I signed up for one year as a labourer, wherever they sent you.

We were ten days at sea, on the *Nelly*, and none of us knew where we were going in Canada, or what work we would do. The last evening, after supper, we were told to assemble in the main hall, and the Canadian officials asked for 200 volunteers to work in the bush in Northern Ontario. Then they called for miners. I waited to hear if they would call for construction workers, since that was the closest thing to my own trade. I

Volksdeutsch immigrant, Canwood, Saskatchewan, 1951.

waited and waited, until there were 150 of us left, and then they said, "All the rest of you are going to Western Canada, to work on the farms."

Half the group was dropped off in Winnipeg, and twenty of us were taken off the train in Regina. It was Sunday afternoon, and they put us up at the old Metropole, near the station.

The next morning, a group of farmers came in and picked us over. I was the second man picked. I was twenty-one years old, and a big man. "Do you know how to milk cows?" was all the farmer asked me.

I spent fourteen months on that farm at Edenvelt, longer than I needed to, because we had only agreed to work for one year. My farmer had an operation after I'd been there eight months, and he took a long time to recuperate. So I stayed on to help.

A lot of the other guys didn't stay for the full year, as they were supposed to. They ran off after a month or so. One of them worked on a neighbouring farm, for a Baptist family, and he was very unhappy because they said there was to be no smoking or drinking at their place. This man found out that I went to town twice a week with the milk, with a team of horses. There were forty or fifty milk cans to move, and he offered to help me. He came in with me, but he didn't come back.

I couldn't complain about my place. Farm work was easier here than in Czechoslovakia, and they paid me top wages — $100 a month in the summer, seventy-five in the winter. And I was able to speak German to the farmer, although his wife was English. After the farmer went into hospital, I had to learn some English fast, to work with his wife. *Czech refugee.*

"I did it the hard way . . . ."

We Polish combatants weren't admitted as immigrants. We came as contract labour, to work two years on the farm for a fixed income of $45 a month. Later, we were told, we could apply for landed immigrant status, but the Labour Department threatened us, "If you don't behave, we'll ship you back."

We were allies, fighting on the side of Canada. When Canadian veterans came home, everything was provided for them — education, training, housing. But we were treated like slaves.

My group was demobilised in St. Thomas, Ontario. We spent the night at a camp there, and in the morning we were lined up for a group of farmers to choose from — just like a slave market. The tallest, strongest men went first. The farmer who picked me took us back to his place at Listowel, near Palmerston, and I was put straight to work cleaning up manure, without a meal, without a chance to change out of my uniform.

It was a 200-acre dairy farm, with twenty-five cows and a hundred pigs, and there were only two people to work it, the farmer and myself. That meant a seven-day week, from dawn to dusk, with Sunday afternoons off. I worked in total isolation. There was nobody to talk to, because nobody visited the farm, so I met nobody who could tell me about my rights. I started work in November, and the first weekend I had off was in April. I spent it in Toronto, asleep in a hotel room.

In the summer of 1947, I made contact with some Polish people in Kitchener, and I decided to go there to look for work, despite my contract. If that farmer had treated me differently, I would have stayed, but I was able to use my damaged hand as a reason for quitting. It was injured in the war, it was shortened, and my fingers were stiff and painful.

In Kitchener, I was told to spend my second year in a hospital as an orderly, for the same $45 a month, but I decided to take a chance, and go my own way. I worked in various jobs, in a factory, as a housepainter, as a bartender and, finally, for Electrohome. I started out on the assembly line and I ended up as a highly qualified technologist.

I've never gotten over the way we were treated when we came to Canada. We were forced by political events to come here, but we weren't peasants, and Canada wasn't a pioneer country any more. A lot of us had education, and the government should have exploited our potential. But they were only interested in our muscles. There was no help for people like me who wanted to get a Canadian degree. I'm not talking about money, grants, but about encouragement and advice — where to go, who to talk to. I did it all, eventually, but I did it the hard way. Not like the people who came later. They had job training, language classes, everything handed to them on a plate. *Polish refugee.*

Polish veteran with employer, City View, Ontario, 1947.

Lumberman's Phrase Book

I am John Schmidt. (Ai em Dschan Schmidt) Ich bin Johan Schmidt.

There are great woods in Canada. (dhahr ahr greiht uuds in Kanada) Es gibt grosse Walder in Kanada.

Mr. Brown is the camp boss. (Misster Braun is dhih kemp boss) Herr Braun is der Lagerleiter.

When do we go to work? (huen duh uih goh tu wohrk?) Wann gehen wir zur Arbeit?

Canada is a great country. (Kanada is eh greht Kontri) Kanada is ein grosses Land.

"A short list of sentences in English and German," issued to immigrant woods workers by the Department of Labour, 1947.

"If you are weaklings . . . ."

It took a while, but in the end we got a sponsor in Port Loring, southwest of Sudbury. He needed a bushworker and a cook, and he said there was room for our small daughter.

He met us at the railway station, and then he took us across the lake and into the bush, and there was this little log cabin near the main camp. This was February, and we had to clear the snow off it to get inside. It had one room with a round stove in it. There was no running water and no outhouse. The only washrooms were in the men's camp.

We were tired, my wife was pregnant, my little girl was crying with the cold. None of us had clothes warm enough for Canada in the winter. Our sponsor's mother came over to see what DPs

Lithuanian bushworkers, Cochrane, Ontario, 1948.

looked like. She looked my wife up and down, and then she said, "She's even got nylon stockings, and she's supposed to be destitute." When I said to the man, "My wife and daughter will want to wash once in a while," he gave us a tin basin. If you are weaklings, you can go under at such times.

Bushwork ended in the middle of March, and the boss told us, "Okay, now you're on your own. Maybe there'll be a job in the sawmill in June." He'd promised us a year's work, and when we complained, he said, "You get out of the bush, you get out of my sight."

I didn't know till later that I could complain to the government. I was scared. I thought if I said anything they might ship me back to Europe. So I was quiet, as quiet as could be. But my wife had a cousin in Sudbury, and he told us INCO was hiring people. You had to weight 140 pounds to work underground, 130 to be a surface worker, and I weighed 125 pounds. So I got a job in Sudbury washing cars for a while, and I ate as much as I could stuff into myself. Next time INCO was looking for surface labourers, I went back again, and this time I weighed 128 pounds, and they took me on. *Latvian refugee.*

"So many of us were educated . . . ."

The worksite we were sent to was northeast of Port Arthur, and it took three days on the train to get there. When we stopped in Montreal and Toronto, we got a hostile reception from Slavic groups who met us there, at the station. "There's nothing here for you to do," they said. "We've just come out of a depression."

The section heads on the railway were old immigrants, from the Ukraine and eastern Europe. They'd come in the 1920s, and they were very bitter, very left wing. They thought we should have stayed to help the Communists, instead of running away, and they gave us hell. The foreman was the most belligerent, and he particularly resented anyone with any schooling. And so many of us were educated people — there were engineers and doctors in our group. Nothing we could do pleased that foreman, not even when he fell off the locomotive and lost his leg, and one of us "no-good-nicks" saved his life by stopping the bleeding.

Eventually, the railway separated the intelligentsia from the others, and they sent us to British Columbia. There were twenty-nine of us, and things were better there. I loved the scenery, the mountains. I came from the Alps.

The first time I was in a house in Canada was in Lytton, B.C. The German pastor there invited all twenty-nine of us to tea. We all spoke German, although we came from many different nationalities. They were so kind to us. We had strawberries and crumpets and proper tea, and they had such nice things there, a china tea service and fine furniture. It was beautiful, so civilised, but we felt so clumsy, so out of place. Already, we walked like bears, a railwayman's walk, which you get because rail ties are set too close together for a tall man's stride. And a Latvian engineer slipped on a carpet and fell right on his behind. It made me realise that, as soon as this year was over, I must find a way of getting back into the kind of society where I belonged. *Slovenian refugee.*

"It's like old times."

The foreman did a lot of shouting and arm waving, for the seventy-four men on the job could not speak English. A few months ago they were displaced persons from Europe.

"It's like old times," said their foreman, Jack Easby. It brought back memories of other times in the history of the Company when young men from Europe, fired with the spirit of a new country, laid rails forward in fast time. Now men from Europe are helping again — this time to replace old rails worn out under heavy war traffic conditions. The men "caught on" quickly and the new rails spread out along the ties at the rate of seventy rails an hour.

Spanner, *Canadian Pacific staff magazine, June 1948.*

Boxcar accommodation for railway construction gang.

Des Joachims hydro-electric power project on the Ottawa River, completed 1951.

Political Arguments

Three hundred and sixty of us were sent in railway cars to the site, to build a powerhouse on the Ottawa River. There were Poles, Ukrainians, Yugoslavs, Hungarians, Russians and more. We lived forty or fifty people to one room, in the barracks, and we got into lots of political arguments with some older immigrants who came to Canada long before the war. They wouldn't believe what the Communists were like in Europe, what they'd done to us. Maybe it was a good thing there was no drink allowed, or we would have got into some violent fights. *Russian refugee.*

Displaced Persons, Des Joachims, 1947.

"Some romantic endings . . . ."

Early in 1947, I was working in a British officers' mess in Germany when one of the officers told me that Canada was looking for girls to go to Canada, to do domestic work. They were looking for a trial group of ten girls, and my sister and I both put our names down. We were told we would have to work for one year, for some prominent people who would sponsor us. I was twenty-five and my sister was eighteen, and we'd been in Germany since 1944. We left Estonia just as the Russian troops moved in.

We could have gone to England, but we wanted to get as far away from the war as we could, and anything that reminded us of it. I'd always thought of Canada as a place to find a husband, with a great surplus of men, all those beautiful rich ranchers out west. And Canada was supposed to have a climate like we grew up with.

We had all kinds of tests, physical and political too: why had we left our own country? what political parties had we belonged to? what had we been doing in Germany? It went on and on.

It was obvious we had to underplay our education. They certainly weren't interested in that, because they really wanted people who would stay on doing domestic work. So the girls who were good at shorthand and typing didn't put that on their application forms. My sister had never cooked or done any housekeeping, she'd just finished school, but she said she had studied home economics. Myself, I had worked in an office in our city hall, but I liked sewing, I was interested in doing hospital work, and I could say I'd done some waitressing in Germany, at the officers' mess.

My sister and I were both chosen to come. All ten girls were either Estonians or Latvians. Five of us came to Ottawa, and that's where we found out who our prominent sponsors were: C. D. Howe (Minister of Reconstruction), Lester Pearson (Minister of External Affairs), Hugh Keenleyside (Deputy Minister in charge of Immigration) and M. J. Coldwell (leader of the CCF Party).

Mrs. Howe wanted two maids, so that's the household where my sister and I went. One of us had to be the cook, she said — which was it to be? Neither of us could cook, but my sister looked so sorry and sad-eyed that I volunteered. And I learned fast. I made my first pie the night Sir Stafford Cripps came to dinner, and Mrs. Howe said it was very good. My only disaster was the fresh garden peas. I'd never used a pressure cooker before, and I couldn't make it work. But there were frozen peas in the fridge, and nobody seemed to notice the difference. Sometimes it was obvious when I got something wrong. I was told to make watercress sandwiches when Mackenzie King came to tea, and I'd never seen watercress before. I didn't chop it, and I put the stalks in the sandwiches, as well as the leaves.

My sister and I had the third floor of this beautiful big house to ourselves, and we were treated well. The only serious problem came when our year was up. Mrs. Howe didn't want us to leave, and when we insisted, she wouldn't speak to us again. The day we left, she wouldn't even come downstairs to say goodbye. But our agreement was for one year, and I wanted to work in a hospital. My sister intended to be a dressmaker.

Newspapers wrote articles about us, because we were the first young girls to come as refugee workers, and our photographs were in all the newspapers. We got lots of marriage proposals by mail. Some said they liked European girls because of their appearance, some said it was our inner strength that appealed. I got one proposal from a hospital orderly, telling me how much money he'd saved by living at home with his mother.

When the girls all got together for coffee, we used to compare our offers of marriage by mail. Nobody accepted one, but there were some romantic endings to our story. The girl who worked for the Keenleysides married their son, and I married a journalist from the Press Gallery who came to write a story about our experiences in that first year in Canada. *Estonian refugee.*

Displaced Persons leaving Halifax, 1947.

IV   Advertising Postwar Canada

T0 ENSURE THAT THE BULK of immigrants would come from Britain and northwest Europe, an active advertising campaign was launched there by the Immigration Branch in 1951. By this time, the fears of a postwar recession had been proven groundless. There was an abundance of work available; on the land, in the forests, on the railways, down the mines, in the factories. Everywhere, it seemed, there were construction projects needing immigrant labour: highways, including the Trans-Canada; new railway lines to tap the mineral resources of Ungava and Labrador; dams for hydro projects in Ontario, Quebec, British Columbia and the Yukon; the St. Lawrence Seaway leading into the Great Lakes, and new harbour facilities at Port Arthur and Fort William; Canada's first subway in Toronto; new towns, like Kitimat, B.C., and, everywhere, new housing. Heavy construction called for male workers, but there were plenty of openings for women in commerce and industry, in agriculture and domestic service. "Canada has more than a million women at work," said one Immigration Branch filmstrip.

Federal advertising about these opportunities tended to be direct and down-to-earth. By contrast, provincial ads were glowing, full of turn-of-the-century hyperbole. "Our streets are not paved with gold but the gold is there for any who are willing to find it," said one Ontario pamphlet, while Alberta's Social Credit government boasted about the province's "black diamonds" (coal) and "liquid gold" (oil), sufficient to supply the world's needs for centuries to come. Calgary and Edmonton, with populations of 100,000 and 115,000 respectively, "may surpass Ottawa and even rival London as a focus of the Empire," said one brash

London, England, 1948.

advertisement, curiously prophetic but, at that time, unrealistic.

The photographs chosen by the Immigration Branch for their filmstrips provide a fascinating, if selective, record of everyday life in postwar Canada. Without any of the flamboyant salesmanship of their turn-of-the-century predecessors, immigration officials set out to present a detailed picture of Canadians at home and at work; on the farm or in the city; at church and at school; shopping or enjoying their leisure time.

Even the most prosaic federal advertising presented a "land of milk and honey" image to Europeans, who had been desperately short of food for years, and to the comparatively fortunate British, whose food had been tightly rationed. There was a bounty of food in so many of the pictures illustrating life in Canada: on the shelves of large groceterias, known as "supermarkets," on farmhouse tables and in city-dwellers' refrigerators, as well as the promise of plenty in the wheat fields and cattle pastures, apple orchards and dairy farms. An atmosphere of cheerful materialism ran through these filmstrips. All the benefits of the "electrical age" were there to make life more convenient: stoves and refrigerators, washing machines and vacuum cleaners. Winter had been vanquished by self-stoking coal furnaces with automatic thermostats, in the cities, at any rate, but the march of progress and electrical wiring was reaching the farmhouse, too. Of course, there was that ultimate symbol of prosperity, the family car.

The picture of Canadian life presented to would-be immigrants left no doubt about the kind of people the government wanted to come to Canada. The photographs came from different provinces, and showed Canadians in many walks of life, but the people in them looked homogeneous. An English expatriate housewife showed off her gleaming new kitchen in Edmonton. A curly-haired child tried on a velvet-collared coat of the kind Prince Charles was wearing at the time. "Church" meant the United Church in Beaverton, Ontario, where the ladies in the congregation wore white gloves and picture hats. Lawn bowling was a favourite form of summer recreation. Afternoon tea was served in Ontario farmhouses.

The text accompanying the pictures did not ignore the "other Canada" completely. The Catholic Women's League and the Young Women's Hebrew Association were mentioned, along with the Young Women's Christian Association, as organizations helpful to newcomers.

Quebec's French-speaking and largely Catholic population was described, and the existence of various ethnic groups acknowledged. But the real message lay in the photographs, and visually, the pictures emphasized, beyond any shadow of doubt, the fundamental character of Canada which Mackenzie King did not want to change.

Life in Canada looked comfortable, but the pictures did not convey the feeling of overconsumption and of excess. Canadians appeared to be healthy, hearty, unpretentious people, with a zest for the outdoors and for simple pleasures like corn roasts and square dances. "Culture" meant the Dominion Drama Festival, regional music festivals and children's art classes. Above all, Canadians were God-fearing and family-oriented, enjoying a church basement "social" or a family picnic in the countryside, using the family car. Families gathered around the radio for the children's bedtime story, or around the piano for a singsong. "The family at home is one of Canada's great resources," said one advertisement, and "neighbourhood friendliness is a Canadian characteristic."

Many of the photographs used in the Immigration Branch filmstrips were almost ten years old by the time they appeared: loggers and factory workers, church-goers and hockey players, among others, had all been photographed during the Second World War. Presumably, the rate of change in the 1940s was not considered sufficient to "date" these pictures, and their use reinforced the impression of a lifestyle which had not altered significantly during and after the war years. To Britons and Europeans, whose lives had been drastically affected by war, the message was as reassuring as it was inviting.

"... 733,000 farms, from ocean to ocean, contribute to the wealth of Canada's leading basic industry. It employs over a quarter of the gainfully occupied population, and over one-third of the gainfully occupied males. Influenced by sea breezes, mineral deposits, great inland lakes, wide prairies and high mountains, types of farming vary greatly throughout the land." *Immigration Branch filmstrip.*

Harvesting on the prairies. The average wage for male farm workers rose from $75, plus room and board, in 1946 to $105 in 1952. Polish war veterans and Displaced Persons were paid $45 a month in the later 1940s.

Railway construction, St. Lawrence-Labrador line to Ungava. In 1952, construction workers earned between $1.00 and $1.50 an hour. Rates were higher in British Columbia than in eastern Canada.

Loggers, western Quebec. In 1952, choppers and cutters in eastern Canada earned an average of $5.40 a day.

Trans-Canada Highway construction, Saskatchewan.

"In the five postwar years, Canada spent $1,500,000,000 on roads and related construction, but there is still a considerable backlog resulting from deferment during the depression years and the Second World War. The 5,000 mile, all-weather, two-lane Trans-Canada Highway alone is expected to cost $300,000,000." *Immigration Branch filmstrip.*

Sawmill, British Columbia. In 1952, the average wage for sawmill employees was $1.90 an hour, but rates ranged widely, from $1.19 in Quebec to $2.42 in British Columbia.

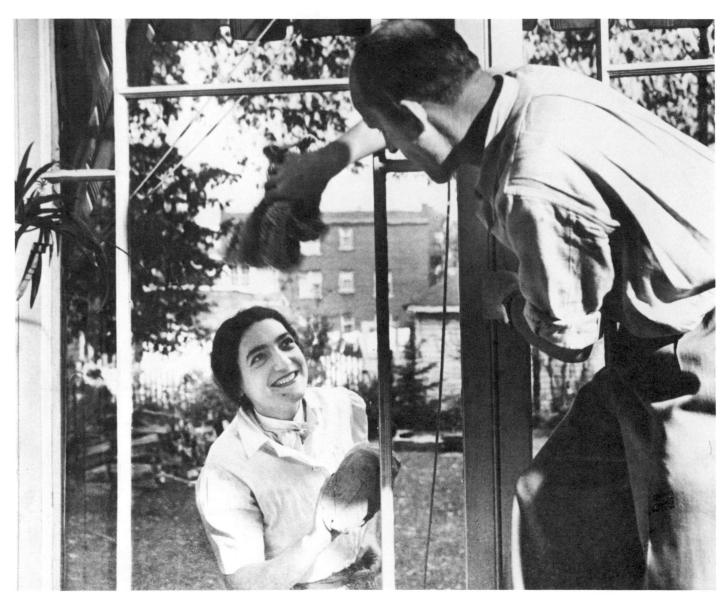

More than 400,000 women worked as domestics in 1952. The average wage was $40 a month, plus board.

"Domestic workers generally live with families, are comparatively well paid, and usually have holidays with pay. Many of them wear uniforms, and as a rule, working conditions are arranged to make their tasks as pleasant and efficient as possible.

Both man and wife work together in the domestic service, one taking over the tasks of a handy-man or gardener, and the other, household care. Domestic employment provides opportunity for newcomers to become familiar with the language and customs of their new community." *Immigration Branch filmstrip.*

Textile industry, Montreal. One-third of all women employed in manufacturing worked in textiles. In 1952, the average hourly rate in rayon and nylon manufacture was $1.13 an hour for male weavers and $1.09 for female. Male spinners earned $1.26 an hour and females 92¢.

"Typists and stenographic 'pools,' spacious offices designed for maximum efficiency, are an important factor in business administration." *Immigration Branch filmstrip.*

Stenographic pool. The average wage for typists was $41 a week in 1952, compared to $24 a week for waitresses.

"Some Canadian cities are big, bustling and modern; some have an old-world flavour inherited from the pioneers, all are growing as Canada develops into an industrial and trading nation." *Immigration Branch filmstrip.*

Toronto, 1940s. In the ten years 1941-1951, Toronto's population grew from 909,928 to 1,117,470. Over the same period, Montreal's population grew from 1,145,282 to 1,395,400.

Houses being Built

Construction of houses in Canada has never quite caught up with the demand, in spite of the record number built since the war. 544,547 units have been completed during the years from 1945 to 1951.

> Life in Canada: "An Introduction." *One of a series of filmstrips produced by the National Film Board for the Department of Citizenship and Immigration, 1951.*

> *(In 1952, the Canadian Labour Congress estimated that Canada was short of 700,000 housing units. — Author)*

No Palaces

The slick-paper magazines lead us to believe that the average family lives in a beautiful, 5-bedroom house on an acre of lawn and garden. But, in reality, the homes that most Canadians live in are not sumptuous palaces. They are likely to be conventional houses on a street with many other such houses. Each house usually has a small lawn, and perhaps some flowers in front, with no hedge or fence separating it from the neighbours. The houses probably have gardens at the back as well. Children in such districts play together and go to school together, and their parents find that they too have many interests in common. Neighbourhood friendliness is a Canadian characteristic. *Immigration Branch filmstrip.*

Winnipeg street. In 1950, the average sale price for a single-family dwelling was $8,883 in Winnipeg, $7,473 in Vancouver. Prices in Montreal and Toronto were $9,633 and $10,151 respectively.

What About a Place to Live?

You may be surprised to learn that a country which experienced no wartime devastation has not enough houses. Canada is, in fact, faced with a grave shortage of accommodation. During and since the war, many families have been forced to live in makeshift and unsuitable quarters. While steps are being taken to meet the situation, there is no use pretending that the problem has been solved.

> This is Canada! *A pocket guide prepared for the Department of Mines and Resources by the Canadian Association for Adult Education, 1948.*

A Woman's Place

Woman's place, it used to be said, is in the home. Few people, perhaps, would agree with this today, now that women have taken their place in occupations that used to be territory for men only. But today as ever, the home is still the most important part of a woman's life.

> Life in Canada: "Women at Home." *One of a series of filmstrips produced by the National Film Board for the Department of Citizenship and Immigration, 1952.*

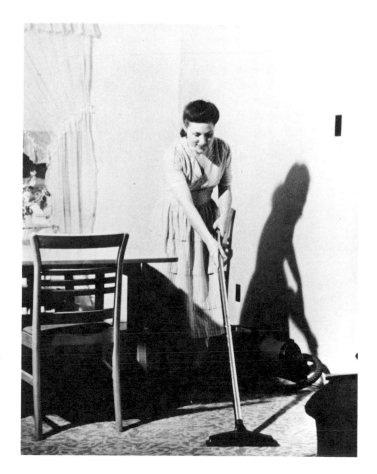

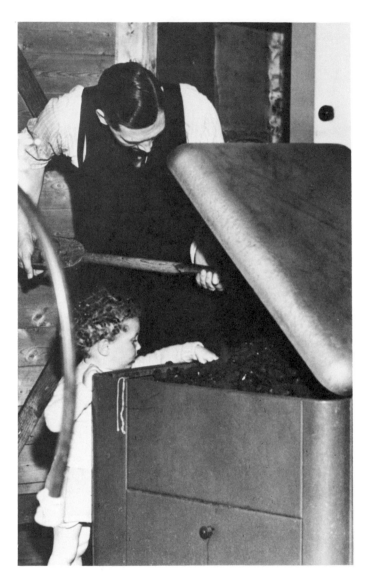

Coal prices varied widely across Canada. In 1952, a ton of coal cost $19 or $20 in Halifax, Winnipeg and Vancouver, $25 in Toronto and $29 in Montreal.

"The most common fuels for city families are coal and oil. Sometimes coal furnaces work by means of an automatic stoker that feeds coal into the furnace. A well-filled stoker can go several days without attention." *Immigration Branch filmstrip.*

"The cold winters in Canada make central heating a necessity. Many houses have automatic furnaces, which are equipped with a thermostat in one of the ground-floor rooms. A flick of the dial controls the heat of the house at the desired temperature, and most housewives wear cotton frocks to work in all winter long." *Immigration Branch filmstrip.*

"In many a farmhouse, one still finds the old-fashioned kitchen in the heart of the household. Wood is plentiful in most parts of the country and is the most common fuel for cooking and heating. The coal-and-wood stove has a built-in tank to provide hot water for most of the family needs." *Immigration Branch filmstrip.*

"Electrification is spreading farther and farther out into the country, so that farm homes are getting more and more city conveniences. The farmer with electricity may boast about his new milking machine; his wife can also boast about her new electric range. Cooking is simpler, and her kitchen cleaner, with electricity." *Immigration Branch filmstrip.*

Beaverton United Church, Beaverton, Ontario. In 1951, out of 14 million Canadians, 6 million belonged to the Roman Catholic Church, nearly 3 million to the United Church, and 2 million to the Church of England in Canada. Presbyterians, Baptists and Lutherans, combined totalled 1-3/4 million.

"The church is the centre of a rich social life for the congregation: boys' and girls' groups, clubs for teenagers, women's auxiliaries, societies for business and professional people . . . all these make church life a family affair. The church provides a friendly meeting place, as well as a place of family worship. After the service comes time for small talk, and perhaps an invitation to Sunday dinner, or a drive in the country." *Immigration Branch filmstrip.*

Smallpox vaccination was standard and effective, but anti-polio vaccines had only recently been developed, and there were 4,755 diagnosed cases of polio in 1951. In 1953, in the most severe polio epidemic ever recorded in Canada, there were 8,734 cases documented. The hardest-hit provinces were Manitoba, with 2,300 cases, and Ontario, with 2,200.

"The health of Canadian children is guarded by immunization centres across the country. But a healthy, happy childhood is still the best insurance against the ills of later life, and Canada, as most newcomers soon realise, is a fine place to bring up children." *Immigration Branch filmstrip.*

"Education is a provincial matter in Canada, so that the school-leaving age differs from province to province. Public school education is compulsory. Public and high school education is free. Technical schools and agricultural colleges offer special training to boys and girls with practical aptitudes." *Immigration Branch filmstrip.*

"The country store combines hardware, grocery, clothing and all other services in one, for it may often be the only store for miles around. Though modern enough to be an agency for the latest in farm and household equipment, the Canadian country store still preserves the odour of the apple barrel and the leisurely tempo of an earlier age." *Immigration Branch filmstrip.*

Retail Prices of Staple Foods by Cities, December 1952.

	Halifax	Montreal	Toronto	Winnipeg	Vancouver
Beef sirloin (1 lb.)	92.0¢	91.6¢	83.5¢	76.4¢	94.0¢
Hamburger (1 lb.)	54.8	48.6	48.4	48.5	56.8
Bread (1 lb.)	12.8	12.0	12.0	14.0	14.9
Sugar (1 lb.)	9.8	9.7	10.0	13.0	10.3
Eggs, Gr. A (1 doz.)	64.8	62.8	57.8	54.8	66.3
Butter (1 lb.)	71.4	64.8	66.8	65.6	69.7
Coffee (1 lb.)	112.4	106.2	101.2	99.5	97.2

Working and Living Conditions in Canada, *Department of Labour publication, April 1, 1953.*

"Many women shop at large groceterias, often called 'supermarkets.' The customer serves herself from the long shelves and pays at the cashier's desk, when she is ready to leave. One advantage of this method of shopping is that it can be done without language, a great help to newcomers whose English has not yet had time to become fluent." *Immigration Branch filmstrip.*

Buying goods on credit. In May 1951, a four-piece Kroehler living room set was advertised in Toronto at $169, and two-piece chesterfield sets at $129.

"Many Canadian families buy expensive things, like furniture and appliances, on the instalment or 'hire-purchase' plan. After a small down payment, they pay off the balance in monthly instalments. Meanwhile, of course, they have had the use of the article while they pay for it." *Immigration Branch filmstrip.*

"Music and drama festivals, bringing Canadians together in friendly competition, play a great part in fostering the cultural growth of this young, enthusiastic country, and help to develop a richer, fuller, more satisfying life for all Canadians." *Immigration Branch filmstrip.*

Manitoba Music Festival, Winnipeg.

"With winter, is heard the ring of skates and the sharp thud of the hockey puck against the boards of the neighbourhood rink. Every vacant lot has its sheet of ice and its own group of would-be hockey stars." *Immigration Branch filmstrip.*

Montreal.

"Many Canadians of all ages spend part of each summer at a cottage beside the water or a resort in the woods. Often, it is possible to live in the country all summer, commuting to work in the city." *Immigration Branch filmstrip.*

"People in Canada still find real enjoyment in the home, whether it is an apartment or a farmhouse. The family at home is one of Canada's great resources."
Immigration Branch filmstrip.

V   The Old Stock

Dutch immigrant family.

T HE MORE WE GET, THE BETTER," said Deputy Minister Hugh Keenleyside, referring to British immigrants in 1949. "We like them to bring a little money with them, but even if they don't, they are welcome. If a Britisher shows up at one of our ports with only a shilling in his pocket, and if he is fit, there is a place for him here and we shall bid him welcome."

Until the new Citizenship and Immigration Department was created in 1951, no vigorous campaign was launched to recruit British (or other) immigrants. The lack of any immediate postwar federal initiative prompted the impatient conservative premier of Ontario, George Drew, to "jump the gun" and organise a provincial airlift of eight thousand Britons in 1947-48, circumventing the trans-Atlantic shipping bottleneck and counterbalancing the "foreigners" being admitted from European refugee camps as sponsored labour. Drew's action annoyed the federal government, which shortly afterwards negotiated a deal with Trans-Canada Airlines, whereby Britons could fly direct to Canada for the considerably lower price they would have paid for their ocean passage.

In terms of assistance to British immigrants, however, Canadian efforts paled by comparison with Australia's vigorous immigration campaign. Launched immediately after the war, with a target of 75,000 a year from the British Isles, Australia offered free passage to former British servicemen and their wives, and almost-free passage to other Britons, who were required to pay a nominal ten pounds ($30) towards the cost. Housing and integration programs were also offered, in contrast to Canada's laissez faire approach.

Between 1948 and 1951, the proportion of Britons among immigrants arriving in Canada declined progressively, despite various schemes launched by private groups: to bring former Indian Army officers, after independence; to bring girls from Britain's wartime Land Army to work on the farms; to bring five-year-old British orphans to a new life in Ontario. These schemes were marginal, of course, and some were eccentric, like one the expatriate Lord Beaverbrook favoured, to shift the centre of the Commonwealth to Canada, through a massive infusion of British immigrants. But the fact remained that Britons constituted only 18.2% of all immigrants to Canada in 1949, and a mere 15% in 1951, the year when postwar immigration peaked, with 194,000 new arrivals, 31,000 of them British.

Various factors played a part in the decline of British immigration, including Australia's energetic recruiting campaign and competition from New Zealand, South and East Africa and the two Rhodesias. There was also an acute shortage of trans-Atlantic shipping, which meant lengthy waits for passage. Probably more serious was the 1948 devaluation of the British pound, from $4.03 to $3.08, accompanied by a severe reduction in the amount of capital an immigrant could transfer to Canada, from £5,000 to £1,000, divided into four yearly installments of £250. This restriction did not apply to sterling-area countries like Australia.

Concern about the declining percentage of British immigrants and the potential "radical change in our population characteristics" began to be heard in parliament and the press, and a variety of groups urged the government to set up an assisted passage scheme. They included the Army, Navy and Air Force Veterans, the Canadian Council of Churches, the Church of England in Canada (later known as the Anglican Church of Canada), the Edmonton Chamber of Commerce, and the Royal Empire Society, which pointed out: "The young married man, with the average family of three small children (considered by immigration authorities to be the ideal settlement unit) can usually raise the approximately $100 now required to get to Australia, but the average of about $650 necessary to get him to a Canadian employment centre is frequently quite beyond his means. The financial consideration dictates his destination, and he is lost to Canada."

The outcry prompted the Immigration Branch to prepare a confidential memorandum to Cabinet on the subject of British immigration, and, in 1951, the government did introduce an assisted passage scheme, available to Britons and northern Europeans. It took the form of a loan, to be repaid in full within two years and, until 1955, available only to heads of families. By that time, 32,000 people had taken advantage of the program. But in the meantime, the number of British immigrants to Canada had increased dramatically. Over 350,000 arrived in the years 1945-1955. In the same period, 101,000 immigrants came from the Netherlands, but the total of all other northwest Europeans from "traditional" source countries was only 51,500.

London, England, 1947. Impatient with the postwar shipping shortage which severely hampered immigration from Britain in the late 1940s, the Ontario government of Conservative Premier George Drew organised an "airlift" to Toronto, 1947-1948. The target was 7,000 British immigrants, but 8,000 arrived under this program. Preference was given to agricultural, mining and construction workers, domestics, skilled industrial workers and technicians. To be eligible, men had to be aged 16 to 40 (later reduced to 35) and women, 21 to 45. All had to be able to pay the $200 airfare and to bring a minimum $225 with them.

A chartered planeload of immigrants leaves Northolt airport, England, as part of the Ontario "airlift." The flight took 26 hours or more, and planes landed at Gander, Newfoundland, to refuel en route to Toronto.

A Harrowing Flight

The BOAC Stratocruiser took fifteen or sixteen hours to make the journey from London, when I came in 1952. We stopped at Prestwick and then at Goose Bay to refuel, before carrying on to Montreal. It all depended on the wind and the weather — if it was really bad you went via Iceland. This was January and very blustery weather. The plane fishtailed, and it creaked quite loudly, just like a ship at sea. Cruising speed was about 215 miles an hour.

There were about a hundred passengers on board and we had fold-down beds, a bit like a train. The main compartment ran the length of the plane, but down below, next to the baggage compartment, there was a small bar, with a circular stairway going down to it. The stewards on board were all male.

When we landed at Goose Bay, it was twenty degrees below zero [Fahrenheit], and we were rushed into an old wooden building while they refueled. There were guards on the door to see we didn't go outside, in case we got frostbite. *Scottish immigrant.*

Male immigrants on the Ontario "airlift" spent their
first night in Canada at the Salvation Army residence
on Jarvis Street, Toronto.

Spurred on by Ontario's initiative, the federal government arranged for Trans-Canada Airlines to fly 10,000 immigrants from Britain to Canada between June 1948 and March 1949. The first to arrive were greeted at Montreal airport by the minister responsible for immigration, James A. MacKinnon, and Col. Laval Fortier, Associate Immigration Commissioner.

Later, in 1950, arrangements were made for immigrants to fly TCA to Canada at the special rate of $160, the equivalent of a tourist class ticket on board ship, when there were vacant seats aboard regular TCA flights. 1,797 people came this way, between December 1950 and March 1951.

Ontario to Bolster British Stock

CP, London, June 27, 1947.
The official announcement from Ontario House said: ''As many continentals and foreigners are now being permitted to enter Canada, we feel that it is essential that we maintain our present percentage of British stock.

''The British race is predominant in Ontario. They settled there originally and played a major part in our growth. English, Scots and Irish have always found a cordial and cooperative welcome, and always will.

''We want to strengthen our small towns, villages, and rural parts, where there is a good healthy full life, in many respects similar to that in Britain.'' *Toronto* Globe and Mail, *June 28, 1947.*

''*Almost anything we wanted.*''

My brother Allan came to Toronto, and he got a job the first morning, repairing aircraft instruments. Then he got a job in Ottawa, at Sperry's.

He wrote back about the cars and the boats and the cottages. It sounded as if they were on the brink of a whole new, exciting way of life, and there were we in a council house [public housing in Britain], with two small children and no great prospects. It seemed that, if we came over, we could have almost anything we wanted. *English immigrant.*

High Standard of Living

The Canadian eats well, but drinks more spirits and less beer than his British counterpart. There is no food rationing in Canada. The Canadian tends to dress less flamboyantly than his American neighbour but not so conservatively as the British.

His origins and traditions are reflected in Canadian politics, education and justice, which all lean towards the British and French models. But the Canadian is primarily a North American. His business, press, sports, trade unions and everyday products follow the United States pattern. The Canadian is a great out-of-doors man.

Canada wants to increase her population, but at the same time, she must maintain her high standard of living. It follows that any immigrants she welcomes must be prepared to give of their best. For anyone who intends to make Canada his home, it is as well to think over the following points:

1. Don't be afraid to learn. Whatever your job is going to be, tackle it with the will to work.

2. Try to understand Canadians.

3. Do not be critical at first or you will be unpopular.

4. Your ability will be judged in Canada on the work you do for your Canadian employer. He is not interested in what you were in Great Britain or any other country. To expect otherwise will lead to disappointment.

To Canada, *Cunard Line booklet, late 1940s.*

Farewell to Scotland

Sailing to Canada was still full of drama in 1953. We left from Greenock on the *Empress of Scotland*, and I was fine until we started pulling away from the dock, and this piper began marching up and down the pier, playing "Will ye no' come back again?" The bagpipes have this heart-wrenching sound. I kept telling myself, "I know I'll see my family again, in a few years." But there they were, getting smaller and smaller as the ship pulled away, and there I was, taking the only grandchild away from two sets of loving grandparents. That little five-year-old was the light of everybody's life. And those damned pipes! I could hear them in my head for the longest time. *Scottish immigrant.*

These Scottish domestics travelled to Canada aboard the *Empress of Canada* in March 1951, under a trial plan which required them to pay only $30 down towards the cost of their passage. The Department of Labour advanced the rest of the fare, which had to be repaid at the rate of $10 a month. Minimum salary was $45 monthly, plus room and board.

Under the Assisted Passage Loan Scheme, introduced in 1951, other badly-needed workers from Britain and northwest Europe also paid $30 down, and repaid the remainder of their ticket cost over a two-year period. 32,000 people had used the scheme by the end of 1955. Until then, it applied only to single immigrants and heads of families.

The *Empress of Canada* passing under the Jacques Cartier Bridge, 1952. Montreal was a major port of entry during the summer months.

Processing immigrants, Halifax, early 1950s. The great majority of immigrants reached Canada by ship in the late 1940s and early 1950s, and Halifax was the main port of entry.

Cornflakes

In the immigration building at Halifax, there were tables with people from all the different church groups lined up, ready for you. I remember the Salvation Army ladies; they gave us envelopes with stamps on them, to write home. And there were commercial people, handing out little gifts. Everybody got a small pack of MacDonald's cigarettes and a small box of Kellogg's cornflakes.

Nobody knew what to do with the cornflakes. We ate them dry and we didn't like them. So lots of people threw them away, and the floor was covered with cornflakes. They crunched under our feet as we walked over them. *Dutch immigrant, early 1950s.*

How I chose Canada

I had eight sons, and in 1947, a lot of young men from my country were sent off to fight in Indonesia. I didn't want my boys to be involved. We had just come out of one terrible war. I had been in the army myself in 1940. I decided to emigrate.

I thought of Australia, but America and Canada had the best farmland. There was a quota for America. It was full already and we would have had to wait, but if we came to Canada, our government would help us, they would pay part of our fare.

Dutch immigrant family, Halifax. In June 1947, the first of 15,000 Dutch farmers and their families came to Canada under the Netherlands Farm Families movement, organised jointly by the Netherlands and Canadian governments. Many families came from areas which had been flooded during the war. All agreed to work for one year as hired help on Canadian farms with a minimum wage of $75 a month for a married man, and $45 for a single man.

We were not allowed to bring much money with us from Holland, so I came for a year as a hired man, for $75 a month. After a year, I could send for my money and buy a farm of my own. *Dutch immigrant, Ontario.*

Dutch immigrant family on board a special train which left directly from Pier 21, Halifax, where immigrants landed.

Colonist Class

The rail journey from Halifax to Montreal occupies approximately 24 hours. Trains from the west leave Montreal and Toronto each evening. They take 2 nights and 1 day to Winnipeg, 2 nights and 2 days to Saskatoon and Regina, 3 nights and 2 days to Calgary and Edmonton, and 4 nights and 3 days to Vancouver.

There are two forms of sleeping car: 'Standard' and 'Tourist.' 'Standard' requires a first class ticket, 'Tourist' a coach class ticket. All long distance trains are equipped with dining cars usable by holders of any class tickets. You can buy quick snacks at station lunch rooms during 10-minute stops, and in some cases you can even cook your own meals in special kitchens provided in colonist cars.

There are colonist cars attached to some trains for western Canada, and these provide sleeping space for holders of colonist class tickets without extra charge. This accommodation has no bedding or blankets supplied, and only provides the passenger with a place in which to lie down.

Rates
from Halifax to Toronto . . . $48 (first) $40 (coach)
from Halifax to Winnipeg . . . $87 (first) $72 (coach) $41 (colonist)
from Halifax to Vancouver . . . $143 (first) $120 (coach) $84 (colonist)

To Canada, *Cunard Line booklet, late 1940s.*

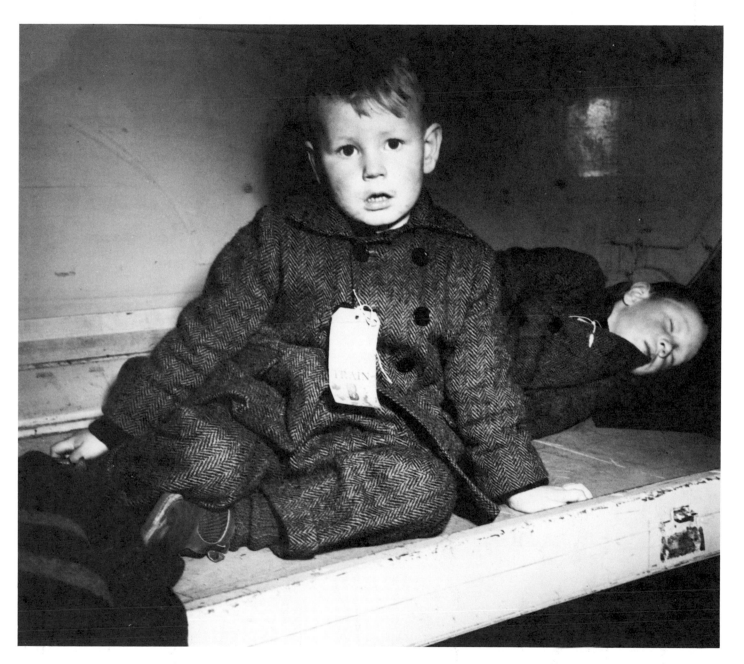

Dutch children in colonist car accommodation.

"We brought very little . . . ."

I had my own business in Copenhagen. I was an electrician by trade. My uncle in Ottawa said, "You'll do well if you come over here," and my wife and I decided we would come. But my father said, "Don't go, my son is my only asset," so we waited three years, until after he died. Then we said, "Now is the time to go." We'd been through a war, and we were afraid of the Russians, what they might do.

My sister came to Canada first. "If you can afford it, fly," she wrote to us from Halifax. She was seasick all the way to Canada. So we flew to Montreal, and we packed most of our things in a big trunk which came by sea. We brought very little with us. We sold all our beautiful furniture because we thought Canada was full of wood, so we could pick up new things for nothing. And then we got here and found out. Oh my God! *Danish immigrant.*

French immigrant family, 1951. In 1948, citizens of France were added to the "preferred" category of immigrants who could enter Canada most easily. The others were British subjects from Great Britain and the white Commonwealth countries and citizens of the United States. But relatively few French immigrants (21,350) had taken advantage of the offer, by the end of 1954.

Danish children en route to Saskatchewan.

The Prairies.

People were the Same

My husband had been in Canada during the war, and after we got married, he brought me to Canada as a bride. He came to buy a garage in Alberta.

We came from Ogden, Utah, and there were 50,000 people in that city. There were only 4,000 or 5,000 people in Raymond, and living condi-tions in the area were not as good as where we came from. Very few houses had bathrooms. And as we drove up, we noticed that the paved road stopped at the border. But there was not much dif-ference as far as people were concerned. *American immigrant.*

British immigrants, 1948.

Italian immigrants on board the *Conte Biancamano*, June 1953.

IMMIGRATION MINISTER J.W. PICKERSGILL was frequently asked about the government's immigration policies in 1954 and 1955, and his replies were often quoted in the press. Speaking to the Toronto Board of Trade in 1955, Pickersgill explained, "We try to select as immigrants those who will have to change their ways least, in order to adapt themselves to Canadian life. That is why frank preference is given to the British, the French and the Americans, and a certain priority is given to the free peoples of Europe. Most people do not want what Mr. King described as a fundamental alteration in the character of our population," he continued, supported by the findings of a February 1955 Gallup Poll, which asked Canadians whether they approved or disapproved of the fact that it was harder for people of some (unspecified) countries to get into Canada than for others. Only 24% said they disapproved, while 59% approved. Among university and high school graduates, the number approving rose to 63%.

"Immigration is a privilege which we have a perfect right to grant or deny as we see fit, and when an alien applies for permission to come to Canada, he is like someone applying for membership in a club," Pickersgill told *Maclean's* magazine in 1955.

Pickersgill had to admit, however, that Canada had not received as many applications for club membership as the government had hoped from certain countries. "Unfortunately," he told the Toronto Board of Trade, "Canada has not been able to attract as many French, Belgian, Danish, Norwegian and Swedish immigrants as we would have liked." Had he given the figures, they would have shown that between 1946 and 1954, only 21,000 French, 11,000 Belgians, 12,000 Danes,

5,000 Norwegians and 2,500 Swedes emigrated to Canada, adding up altogether to a modest 51,500, out of a total of well over one million. Another group on Pickersgill's and King's priority list, the Americans, were represented by 72,000 newcomers.

True, by far the largest group of immigrants, 366,000, came from the British Isles and white Commonwealth countries, despite the temporary downturn between 1948 and 1951. And immigration from the Netherlands had been satisfactorily high, with 101,000 people, many of them coming through the successful "farm family settlement scheme," sponsored jointly by the Netherlands and Canadian governments. But the Dutch were outnumbered by 115,000 Germans who arrived in large numbers after their "enemy alien" status was removed in 1951. And close behind, numerically, came 104,000 Poles and 112,500 Italians, traditionally "non-preferred" groups from eastern and southern Europe.

Walter Harris and J. W. Pickersgill, the St. Laurent Ministers of Citizenship and Immigration, regularly harked back to Mackenzie King's determination not to alter "the fundamental character of the Canadian people." In its original context, this statement referred to Asian immigration, and, as Pickersgill said many years later, "It was a euphemism for a white Canadian policy, only we were too polite to put it that way."

In the early 1950s, entry quotas for three Asian Commonwealth countries were established by Orders-in-Council. One hundred and fifty Indians, one hundred Pakistanis and fifty Ceylonese were to be admitted annually. For all other Asians, special permission was needed. In the case of Japan, no immigrants were allowed until "enemy alien" status was removed in 1952, and in the following three years only 124 Japanese entered Canada.

After the repeal of the 1923 Chinese Immigration Act in 1947, many Canadian Chinese applied for naturalization, which allowed them to bring their immediate relatives to Canada. But frequently, immigration officials were uncooperative.

The "legitimacy" of children born to concubine wives in China, and the difficulty of establishing the age of a child when no documents were available, led to interminable delays, and sometimes to court cases. One particular case, which received press coverage, ended in tragedy. An elderly

Chinese immigrants. In 1947, for the first time in 24 years, Canadian citizens of Chinese origin were allowed to bring their wives and unmarried children into Canada. The majority of Chinese residents were not citizens, but in 1947, they became eligible to apply for citizenship. By the end of 1954, 8,785 Chinese immigrants had arrived.

Chinese cook, who became a Canadian citizen in 1951, applied to bring his eighteen-year-old son by a concubine wife to join him. After lengthy delays, Leong Hung Hing's case went to court, and eventually to the Supreme Court, which ruled, in December 1953, that the son was legitimate. But immigration officials continued to "investigate" the boy, who was now approaching the cut-off age of twenty-one. And then, in December 1954, the father died, and his son was no longer eligible for admission.

Blacks were not mentioned specifically in Mackenzie King's policy statement, and no quotas were subsequently established to allow even a token number into Canada. Close relatives of black Canadians were admissible in theory, but in practice, they experienced considerable difficulties. Their supposed inability to adapt to Canadian "climatic conditions" was used to justify their exclusion, but one such case, involving the Barbadian granddaughter of a Canadian citizen, was raised in the House of Commons by CCF Member Joseph Noseworthy, and caused so much protest that the phrase "climatic conditions" disappeared from the immigration regulations the following year. Apart from black students entering Canadian universities and colleges, the door was virtually closed until 1955, when the insatiable demand for domestic servants led the government to admit one hundred Caribbean blacks a year.

When, in 1955, *Maclean's* magazine reporter Fred Bodsworth charged that Canada's immigration policy was, in fact, discriminatory, Pickersgill was unruffled. "We call it being selective," he told *Maclean's*, "but I do not understand there is any real difference between the words selection and discrimination."

Married by Proxy

My fiancé came to Canada from Calabria in the 1930s. We had wanted to get married before he left, but I was the second daughter in my family, and my older sister had to be married before me. That was the way it was then. So I waited two years, and then I was married by proxy in 1939. Mario could not afford to come back to Italy for the wedding, but he had saved enough for my ticket to Canada. When the war began, I couldn't leave Italy, and Mario never got the money for my ticket back.

During the war, we sent messages to each other

500 Italian immigrants, Montreal, March 1951. Italy's "enemy alien" status was lifted in 1947, and by the end of 1954, 115,000 Italian immigrants had arrived, forming the third largest immigrant group in the immediate postwar years.

through the Catholic Church, and just as soon as it was possible after the war, Mario sent me the money for my plane ticket.

I flew to Halifax, and Mario was at the airport to meet me. He was a young man when I last saw him, when he left for Canada so many years ago, but I recognised him immediately. *Italian immigrant.*

"You work hard and you save."

My older brother came to Canada first, and he worked in the north, on the railway and in the lumber camps. Two years later, he got work in Toronto, building houses, and he sent for his wife and the children. Then they sponsored me — it is the Italian custom. All our family would come to Canada in time and live together in Toronto — my younger brothers and sisters, and my mother.

My sister-in-law wrote such exciting letters home. "There is so much money to be made here," she said. "You work hard and you save. We all live together, and later you can have anything, everything you want."

I dreamed of America, like it is in the movies. I see myself with a beautiful car, with a beautiful girl in a long dress, a fur coat. I see beautiful houses in marble and concrete. I see richness. I dreamed all these things, but I came to Toronto as a labourer, a construction worker. *Italian immigrant, 1952.*

Mothers with Small Children

My husband's parents were living in the United States. They had gone there before the war. But after the war my husband and his brother weren't allowed to join them. They were over twenty-one, you see, by then, and they were married. So my husband's parents said, "Go to Canada, you will be close to us, and one day we may all get to live in the same place."

My husband enquired, and he was sponsored by a general contractor to do brick work and masonry, and painting too. It was arranged through our family. We sailed from Naples to Halifax, on a ship that was full of men coming to work in Canada.

In Halifax, my husband left me with the two small children and our luggage, while he went to see the immigration officer. While I was waiting, a woman in uniform came over to us, and she tried to take my children away. Or I thought so. "No! No!" I said. "No! Go away!" I didn't understand that she was a Red Cross worker, and she wanted to show us that there was a changing room for mothers with small children.

My husband was gone a long time, and we missed the train. There wasn't another one that day, so they let us sleep in the immigration building. But they separated us. My husband took the older boy, and I took Dominic, the baby. But Dominic did nothing but cry all night. He was hungry. My milk had dried up because I couldn't eat on the boat, so he cried. And there were all these strange women there, all different languages, trying to sleep. And to make it worse, I could hear my big son crying for me in the men's dormitory.

I was glad to get on the next train, at 6:00 a.m. *Italian immigrant.*

So Big, So Safe

We were short of everything in Germany after the war . . . food, and clothes, and jobs and places to live. Our country was divided, and we thought it had no future. We were afraid the Russians would move in.

Canada seemed so big, so safe, so far away from our troubles. *German immigrant, 1952.*

German immigrants, Toronto, 1952.

Joey Smallwood's Generosity

I had been in broadcasting in Germany before the war, in television. At the 1936 Olympics, I helped carry the cables, when I was fresh out of school. I was an officer in the German Air Force during the war, and I was taken prisoner by the British. For two years after the war, I worked for the British Forces Network, as a sound engineer, and I also worked as a soundman for North American film companies when they came to Germany. That was how I came to be approached by someone from Newfoundland.

Someone in the Newfoundland government wanted to start up a film studio, Atlantic Films it was called, and they recruited a group of us, all different nationalities, Germans, Latvians and Lithuanians, to go to St. John's. It was January 1952 when we got there, and it was very depressing coming from Europe. St. John's was just a fishing village to us. But we stayed for a while in a hotel, all expenses paid, and that first Christmas [Premier] Joey Smallwood invited us to his house. He wanted to do something for us. *German immigrant.*

German family about to leave for Canada, 1953. 148,500 Germans and Austrians arrived between 1950, when an Order-in-Council removed Germans from the "enemy alien" category, and the end of 1954. Germans were the second largest group of postwar immigrants, after the British.

A P.O.W. Returns

I was sent to Canada as a prisoner of war in 1940, and I liked it here. I'd been in the German navy, in submarines, and I was caught off Helgoland. They sent me to work in Kenora, in pulp and paper, and I ended up on a farm in Manitoba. I wanted to stay, but they wouldn't allow that. They sent us home in December 1946, but out of 1,100 prisoners, 800 wanted to stay.

I asked about coming back as an immigrant, but there was no chance till 1951, when Germans were welcome again. I came through the Baptist Church. You had to sign a paper, and the Church found a farmer to hire me and my wife, for $50 a month. *German immigrant, 1951.*

A Blue Light in the Window

Father had spent part of the war in the United States, as a prisoner of war, and he liked North America. When he went back to Germany after the war, he told my mother about the possibilities. In 1951, we would have had a long wait to get into the United States, but Canada would take us.

To find out about living conditions in Canada, Father went to see the commanding officer of the Canadian troops stationed in Hamburg. A sergeant-major came over to our house on New Year's Day to tell us what food would cost, what rents were like and what things to bring. When we came, we brought practically nothing but our pots and pans, our glassware and a complete set of china. No furniture. How we wished we had, later.

We sailed on an Italian ship, an old troopship, 12,000 tons. Gran and Grandpapa came to see us off, and I couldn't understand, for the life of me, why they were crying. I was nine at the time. They felt they were too old to come with us.

When we got to Halifax, we went through customs, and one of the officers said, "Where do you come from?" My father told him East Prussia, and he said, "Ah, Prussians are Nazis." From then on we called ourselves Germans.

We took the train from Halifax to Montreal, and at night every house seemed to have a strange blue light in the window, very cold looking. We learned much later that those were television sets. *German immigrant.*

Maltese family at Montreal Central Station, November 1948. 500 immigrants from the Mediterranean island arrived that year, under a special agreement between the Canadian and British governments. Malta had been an important British naval base during the war.

"No faces . . ."

After the war time, I saw books about Canada, with pictures of this large country. But there seemed to be no people here, just farms with lots of wheat growing, forests with lots of trees, mountains with lots of snow. Even for the cities, for Montreal, they showed the big buildings, the ships in the harbour, but no people. No faces, no Canadians. What would they be like, I wondered? *Greek immigrant, Halifax.*

Greek family, Montreal.

Hungarians, Montreal, 1948.

Russian family, Ottawa.

"Wherever he goes, I must go."

I am Japanese and my husband is Japanese, but my husband was born in Canada. His father took him to Japan after the war.

My husband's father was a fisherman. He came to Canada in 1910, and he was in the Canadian Army in the First World War. He was wounded and they gave him a pension, but during the Second World War the Canadians locked him up in a camp and separated him from his children. He was very angry, very upset, and after the war he went back to Japan with all his children.

My husband didn't want to go. He said Canada was his country. But he was only a boy, and his father insisted. They would return to help Japan after Hiroshima. They worked very hard, but they never settled down completely, and my husband always wanted to come back here. He found a way in the Korean War. The Canadian Forces had a base in Japan, and he worked for them as an interpreter. Then he enlisted in the Air Force.

He met me in Japan, and we were married before he was posted to Edmonton. He asked for Vancouver, but that was not possible. I spoke no English, and I didn't know what to expect, after the way Canadians treated his father. My family and friends were quite upset, but I wasn't afraid. I said, "Wherever he goes, I must go. He will protect me." But I bought jewellery before I came, so I could sell it, if need be, to help us survive. And I asked my husband for a pearl, on my wedding anniversary. I didn't tell him I wanted it so I could sell it. *Japanese immigrant.*

Couldn't Leave Father Behind

My mother was born in Canada, but she went on a visit to Japan just before the war, and she could not come back here for many years. So after the war, my grandparents went back to Japan, and my grandfather died there.

After my mother married, she had two sons, and she applied to come back to Canada with my father, my brother and myself. It was decided that my mother would come back first, with my grandmother, to establish themselves. They ran a small grocery store in Vancouver.

But when the time came for us to come, the immigration doctor found that my brother had trachoma, so he could not be admitted to Canada. After much delay, I was given a special permit to come by myself, because my father had to stay to look after my brother. But when my brother was cured, my father started to say that he wouldn't come, because he didn't speak English. Time went by, and then the authorities said my brother couldn't come without an escort, and that one special permit for a family was enough.

My mother could not afford to go to Japan to fetch my brother. She had a lawyer, a kindly man, who said the only way to get my brother over here was if she had sole custody. So my parents got divorced. But more time went by before my brother was allowed to come, and at last, he said it was not fair to leave my father who was getting old. He would stay in Japan and look after him. *Japanese immigrant.*

These Japanese Canadians from British Columbia were emigrants, not immigrants. Faced with the choice of resettlement east of the Rockies or repatriation to Japan, nearly 4,000 chose to leave for Japan in 1946, angry and resentful over the Canadian government's confiscation of their property, and their internment during the War.

East Pender Street, Vancouver, 1951.

"Not a tangible community asset . . ."

Generally speaking, coloured people, in the present state of the white man's thinking, are not a tangible community asset, and as a result, are more or less ostracized. They do not assimilate readily and pretty much vegetate at a low standard of living. Many cannot adapt themselves to our climatic conditions. To broaden the regulations would immediately bring about a large influx of coloured immigrants. Quite realistically, this would be, in my opinion, an act of misguided generosity.

A. L. Jolliffe, Director of Immigration, to his Minister's private secretary, October 12, 1949.

"An act of faith . . ."

Canadians don't realise it, but this country got the "creme de la creme" of bright young middle-class West Indians from the British Islands in the early fifties. We came in as students. That was about the only way West Indians could get in at the time. This was before the domestics came. It was easier to get into Canada than the United States, because we were British subjects.

When I got to Kingston, Ontario, I was just a nice light-brown-skinned Catholic boy from Trinidad, bending over backwards to be friendly, and I didn't recognise racial discrimination when I found it. I was looking for a place to stay, and somehow it always seemed as if the room had just been rented, half an hour before I got there.

Eventually, I asked the University for help, and I got a room all right. I shared it with a Bermudian student. Later I found out that Queen's had two

100 black domestics from the Caribbean were brought to Canada under a special government program in 1955, 75 from Jamaica and 25 from Barbados. In following years, the program was extended to other islands.

lists for accommodation, one for whites and one for non-whites. At that time, the University took listings from people who didn't want certain kinds of tenants.

To get into University, you had to pay your fees in advance, which my family did, and you were supposed to provide evidence that you could support yourself, but that was another matter. I was broke by the end of November. I joined the track team, because they gave you a free breakfast, and I had a small job preparing cultures in a lab, but it wasn't enough to keep me. "Well," I said, "if you need money, you go to a bank." My friends thought I was crazy, but the manager at the Bank of Commerce listened to me, and he lent me $300 to get me through the year. It was an act of faith, and you don't forget help like that. I was doing well in organic chemistry, and that summer, when I couldn't find a job, the chemistry professors pooled their funds to create work for me. *Trinidadian immigrant.*

Jamaican soldiers, Canadian Army, early 1940s. West Indians who enlisted for overseas service were eligible for landed immigrant status after the war.

"The first black family . . ."

One of the few ways West Indians could get into Canada in the 1940s was to join the army. If you served overseas in the war, you could come to Canada afterwards — if you hadn't been shot, that is.

My dad worked for Canadian National Steamships, on the boats that went back and forth from the West Indies, and he joined the Canadian Army in 1939. In 1945, he came to Montreal, and he started out in the dry-cleaning business.

He didn't bring us right away from Jamaica because he couldn't find a home, a decent place for us to stay, just run-down housing around St. Antoine, where the other blacks lived. So he kept on sending money home, and after a while he started a dry-cleaning business in Ottawa. Then he rented a house for us in Hull. It was a cheaper place to live.

We had no trouble getting in and finding a job here. I'd been studying medical technology in Jamaica, and my sister had just finished her nurse's training. But we were the first black family in Hull, and people didn't quite know how to treat us. I'd be introduced as "an educated man, not the average black person you read about." *Jamaican immigrant.*

Aircraft production, Montreal.

THE KEYSTONE OF MACKENZIE KING'S 1947 immigration policy statement was the selection of immigrants according to Canada's absorptive capacity, but the government of the day lacked the means of determining that capacity precisely. Consequently, the intake of immigrants varied from year to year, according to the level of employment. The on-again, off-again approach to immigration, or the "tap theory" as it became known, reflected the Department of Labour's concern over unemployment, but frustrated the Department of Citizenship and Immigration's desire for a longer-term approach. The two departments were frequently at loggerheads during this period.

Inevitably, there was an unsatisfactory time lag involved in turning the immigration "tap" on and off. Often, immigrants recruited during a particularly prosperous period did not arrive until the urgent demand had slackened, and then, once the tap had been turned off, employers found it took a frustratingly long time to turn it on again. What was needed, said both employers and labour unions, was reliable, long-range planning, but how to achieve it was a question no one seemed able to answer. The economist Mabel Timlin concluded that frequent, pragmatic tests of economic indicators were the only answers. Sociologist John Porter, concerned about the general lack of social research and planning, admitted in the CCF magazine *Comment*, in September 1952, that predicting future investment trends in Canada was "something like trying to predict the exact course of a golf ball from the first tee to the eighteenth hole."

On occasion, it was inevitable that immigration led to serious unemployment problems. There were almost half a million unemployed in the winter of 1953-54, but this was largely a seasonal problem, and the situation improved rapidly in the spring of 1954. Generally speaking, the early fifties were very prosperous years, and the "tap" was "on" much more than it was "off." Almost 682,000 immigrants entered Canada between 1951 and the end of 1954, bringing total postwar immigration to 1,112,470.

English immigrant farm worker, Ontario, 1947.

"Father never complained."

Father had been in the wine business in Hungary, but to get us admitted to Canada, he had to promise to buy a farm, and to send money ahead for this purpose. When we arrived, he looked at vineyards in Niagara and then at tobacco farms in Tillsonburg, and he decided on tobacco. It was the biggest cash crop in Ontario at the time. You could buy a farm for a small down payment, and each year a quarter of the crop went towards the purchase price.

He started farming with one hired hand, sowing the seed and running the tractor, and he had a very good crop. But he soon realised his farm was too small to be really profitable, so he bought a bigger one. Then, in October, he decided to buy a car. He thought a Plymouth was too tiny, so he bought a Chrysler, as big as a locomotive to our European eyes.

Father had never driven before. He had always had a chauffeur at home, so he asked me to bring the car into the middle of a field. It was after the harvest, the land was flat, and there was a light frost on the ground, but no snow. Father said, "Just give me an explanation," so I drew a diagram of the dashboard on a shirtboard.

In three weeks, he taught himself to drive, and he went to the police for a test, and passed that with no trouble. He was sixty-three years old, and that year, he learned enough English to read the whole *New York Times* from front to back.

Father never complained. The closest he came was when someone asked him his opinion of Ontario wines. "Well, I've tried them," he said, "and they haven't done me any harm." *Hungarian immigrant.*

When You have no Choice

You are enterprising when you have no choice, and that's the way it was with me, after my husband's accident.

We were working on a farm in Manitoba, and once the seed was sown, the farmer said my husband could go to Kenora for a few weeks, to cut pulpwood. But on the second day, he broke his leg, badly, and he was in hospital a long time. And the farmer said we couldn't stay on at his place.

Paul got Workmen's Compensation for his accident, but it wasn't very much, he'd only been working such a short time. So I found a room in Morris for me and the two boys. I couldn't go out to work because the kids were so small, so I knitted for people. Sometimes they'd pay me with food instead of money, but that was okay. We were never hungry. We could live on very little. I bought day-old bread for 5¢ a loaf, and local farmers would sell me chickens for 50¢, if I plucked them myself.

When Paul got out of hospital, we moved to the city, and he got a job as a welder, 65¢ an hour, then 70¢, and soon he was running a machine shop, earning good money. In sixteen months we had paid off the $800 we owed to the Baptist Church for our fare. *German immigrant.*

"In the beetfields . . . ."

In the beetfields, you covered your head with a scarf and then a hat, because of the hot sun. You covered your arms with long sleeves, because of the mosquitoes.

My sister thought we would never walk upright again — we were always bent over. First, you thin out the row, then you weed, and then you thin again by hand. At harvest time, a tractor loosened the beets so you could pull them out of the ground, and you were bent over again.

All the big families went to the beetfields. We went to work in Coaldale, two weeks after we got to Alberta, thinning out the beets with a hoe. There were seven of us in the fields — five boys, my father and me. Mother and the two youngest girls stayed home.

We lived in a shack to start with, all of us in two small rooms, with no water and no power. But in November, we moved into a small house. Our things had come from Holland, in this big crate, and father made it into part of the house. He made a lean-to out of it, and we put the stove in there.

The second year, my father and the boys worked at the High River airport, and at a factory, building army huts. If you could hammer a nail, you got $1.25 an hour. All the money went home to Mum. There was only one pot in our family! Four years later we rented a farm at Balzac, three-quarters of a section, and then we moved a few miles and rented a whole section, then two-and-a-half sections.

My father never owned a farm, and most of my brothers left for the city. But my oldest brother is still a farmer, and he owns his own place. *Dutch immigrant.*

Very Human and Real

As one fresh from the classroom where you have lived a sheltered life, situations will confront you that seem rough and uncouth, but nevertheless very human and real. Does it jar on you a little? It should not, for instead of mixing with fellow students in the classroom, you are now employed with men, many of whom from early years have been at manual work — life and its bumps, in their case, have been very real. But if they can meet life in its varying aspects, why should the man be nonplussed who comes from a good home, reared with care, and blessed with university attainments. Can you, with your accomplishments, sit with men where they sit? Can you enter and share their thoughts and questionings? If not, then something is wrong in your own training and preparation for life.

Always keep in mind that as a labourer-teacher you are to convey to the men some of your own fine background and attainments you have had in the university. *Instructions to Labourer-Teachers, Frontier College, 1951.*

What I Had Dreamed About

At the end of the war, the Canadian soldiers in Normandy said to me, "Why not come to Canada?" I was just a boy, but the temptation was there. It was always Canada. I dreamed of doing what people in the nineteenth century did, of going off to find a pass through the mountains to the sea. In 1953, I was working for my father, in the fruit and vegetable business, and I wasn't happy. I decided to come to Canada. It was very easy to get in.

I landed in Montreal, and I stayed awhile, but I really didn't like it. They were not enthusiastic about the French from France. They had something against you. I think French people are allergic to other French people. So I went back to the Immigration Office and they said, "If you don't like it here, why not Ontario?"

So I went to work on the CPR for two months, near Kapuskasing, and I liked that — no more city, just lakes and forests, and all kinds of immigrants — Germans, Italians, Poles. In October, many of them decided to go back to Montreal, but one of the Germans said to me, "Why not Vancouver?" So we took the bus from Winnipeg, and as we came over the bridge and I saw Vancouver for the first time, I said, "This is where I'll die."

I had no special trade, so I did various jobs, and I slowly ran out of money. I was working in the kitchen, in an Italian restaurant for a while, and then I met a man who worked in the lumber industry on Vancouver Island. I went over to get a job in a lumber camp there, and to me the island was a paradise! The sea, the mountains, the scent of flowers. There were so few people, though, you could find the tracks of a wolf. It was a virgin place, what I had dreamed about as a boy in France.

I learned to cook, to bake, and I got taken on at one of the smaller camps. I loved the life, and I liked the people. The majority were Canadian-born. There were some French Canadians, as boom men, there were Swedes and a lot of Germans, but the backbone of the business was Anglo-Saxon. I like Anglo-Saxons. I know where I stand with them. With the French, I don't know. The Anglo-Saxon has a simpler mind. *French immigrant.*

Frontier College instructor, teaching English to immigrants on railway gang, 1953. The College, founded in 1899 as the Reading Camp Association, sent university students out each summer as labourer-teachers in mining, lumber, hydro-electric and railway construction camps. There were 48 Frontier College labourer-teachers at work in 1953.

Immigrants Pulled Together

There was a mad rush to check out the map, when we heard we were going to work on the railway in northern Ontario. Twenty-seven of us from our camp all travelled together, first on the ship and then on a special train full of "DPs" — that's what they called us. I'd been a clerk in a general store during the war, but some of the others were professional people. We all started out here the same way.

The train dropped us off in Sudbury, and immediately they put us on another train to Hagar, nineteen miles east. We found the work train there, with three coaches as living quarters, each with ten bunks apiece, one up, one down. At first, I was very disappointed, because my bed was worse than the one I had in camp, but the food was excellent, and the foreman treated us decently. Both the foreman and the sub-foreman were French Canadians.

We moved around, from Hagar to Minnow Lake, changing ties and laying new steel. There were lots of mosquitoes, lots of blackflies, lots of heat. We worked hard, and we made our own rules — lights out at 10:00 p.m., and nobody talked after that.

The twenty-seven of us Yugoslavs stuck together. We were all Catholics, and we told the cook, "It's no use cooking meat for us on Friday, because we won't eat it." That cook was really nice, and on Saturday she'd say, "Okay boys! Who's going to Church tomorrow?" If there was a church anywhere near, she'd pack us a picnic lunch, and on Sunday we would walk miles along the track to the nearest church. There, we could feel at home. The service was all in Latin then, and wherever you went, it was universal.

There were no women, period, on the work train, except the cook and her daughter. When we got to a town, there were all kinds of women, but it didn't do us any good, we couldn't talk to them. We didn't know enough English. And at that time, I wouldn't have considered going with a girl of a different nationality. I was all set to find one of my own.

In 1948-49, we had no clothes except what we'd brought from the camp. What money we earned, we spent on food parcels home. It didn't take long for people on the street to figure out you were a DP. They were curious, but quite friendly. They'd ask, "Where do you come from? How do you like Canada?"

Most of our group left after their year was finished, but I stayed with the railway for another year and a half, and I got promoted to section hand, at 74¢ an hour. But finally I got tired of being shipped around by the CPR, and I got a job with INCO in Sudbury, as a labourer. I still didn't have a girl, but a few months later, I met my future wife in Toronto, at a Slovenian wedding.

She was a refugee from my own country, and she was working at Eaton's, sewing, for $25 a week. When we got engaged, the girls she worked with gave her a shower. She was so happy, she couldn't believe it. She had no possessions, nothing to bring with her to Sudbury. Those girls even called a taxi to take all her gifts home.

We got married in Toronto, and we took a sleeper on the train to Sudbury for our honeymoon. When we arrived, there was a wonderful present waiting for us. My workmates had bought her a sewing machine. *Slovenian immigrant.*

Italian railway workers, Picton, Ontario, 1954.

A Winter in Camp

We didn't know how to cut wood, at first, when we were sent to work for Abitibi, near Lake of the Woods, but we learned fast. It was one of the most peaceful, least demanding periods of my life. We lived army-style, the food was always ready, the laundry was done for us. The organization at that camp was tremendous. I thought, ''If we find all this organization in the bush, what will we find in the city?''

Our morale was very good, very high that winter. The first Christmas card I sent home was made of silver birch bark. That Christmas, our group chopped down a tree and brought it into the bunkhouse. We went to First Aid to get cotton dressings and we strung them on the tree. The Canadians looked at us as if we were cuckoo.

There were cultivated people in that camp, architects and lawyers, and they were very excited when one day a lumberjack came walking into the place with a violin case in his hand. But he was a French Canadian fiddler, and we were so disappointed. But then we started to laugh, to enjoy his style.

Someone in that camp tried to teach us some English, on a voluntary basis, and he tried to explain when to use ''h'' and when not to. He called me out to write on the board, and by great misfortune, I wrote, ''God Shave the King.'' Everybody started to laugh, and I said, ''To hell with this.'' I left his class and I never went back. But I learned, anyway.

In April, we were asked, ''Who wants to leave?'' I left and I went to work for the CNR on a steel gang, near Port Arthur, then Gravenhurst. I changed rails, all the way from North Bay to Toronto, for 83¢ an hour.

One day, the boss said, ''Can you read? Can you write? Then come and work in the office for me.'' I did well there, and in 1951, I was paid $250 a month and my expenses, to inspect all the different work gangs. My job was to solve problems between the company and the immigrant workers. There were human mistakes which led to trouble — worms in the food, and mail from home which went astray. But there was also a crooked contractor who brought people from Italy to work on the railway. He advanced them money to come, but he made too much himself out of them. *Italian immigrant.*

Immigrant workers, 1953.

Loggers.

"All we knew were long hours . . . ."

I was twenty-six when I came out of the army, after the civil war in Greece. I wanted to come to Canada, but I didn't know English, and I had no skills to offer. I'd finished high school, but the war cut off my education. So I came here the same way many other people came — a Montreal restaurant owner paid my fare, on condition that we paid it back out of our wages.

We worked long hours, so we couldn't go to night school to learn the language. We didn't know about minimum wages, unemployment insurance or labour unions. We didn't know the doors where we could go and ask for help, because the social agencies weren't geared up to help us. All we knew were long hours, and working seven days a week.

But we knew enough to leave as soon as we'd paid off our fare. That took me a year and a half. Then I went to Halifax, to work in another Greek restaurant where they paid better, and two years later, my partner and I opened our own place. *Greek immigrant.*

Adapted Well

My seventeen-year-old sister was the second girl in my family that we sponsored, and she went to work in a restaurant. She didn't speak much English, and a man might ask for a steak sandwich, and she'd bring him a sirloin with all the trimmings. But she'd laugh, and he'd laugh — it was all a joke. And the restaurant kept her on, they loved her. She adapted just like that.

What a contrast to my eldest sister. She still speaks terrible English, she never got a good job, she's still working in a laundry, and she's never married. The rest of us all made a go of it here. *German immigrant, Halifax.*

"He was very shy . . . ."

As long as you knew the menu, you could manage. I had no English when I started working in this restaurant in Port Arthur, so I learned the menu by heart.

One young man came every night for his dinner, and I always took his order, without any trouble. Then one night, he asked me for something I didn't understand. It was not on the menu. When I called out to the cook to help, this boy said, "No! No!" but it was too late, the cook came over and he had to explain. That poor boy was asking me out to a show. He was very shy, and he never came back, though I hoped he would. *Finnish immigrant, Northern Ontario.*

No Protection for Domestics

I was always hungry that year I worked as a maid. They were a middle-class family. They certainly weren't poor, but they were concerned about every penny they spent on food. Mrs. Brown would buy one pound of meat to feed six people. I would cook the meal, and then the family would eat in the dining room. Whatever was left, I got to eat later in the kitchen, but there was never enough.

My sister was working for another family nearby, and she used to bring me leftovers from their household. I was so disgusted, I said to my sister, "I survived the war years in Europe, and now I'm starving in Canada, in the land of plenty."

My sister asked me why I stayed on, and when I thought about it, I was sure no Canadian would work in those conditions. I didn't know who to complain to, so I went looking for another job, and I got taken on as a nurse's aide. It wasn't domestic work that upset me, it was the way they treated me. You have no protection doing housework in a strange country, when you don't speak the language well. *German immigrant.*

"They were kind to Japanese."

I never worked before, in Japan, but in Edmonton I went to work in a sewing factory. I started on a big press machine, but I was too short. Every time the steam came out, it came in my face, and I got bad nosebleeds. After that, I worked on a sewing machine for a sportswear manufacturer, and everyone was nice there. They were kind to Japanese. I worked there until I was pregnant. *Japanese immigrant.*

Part of a Big Family

My mother and I both worked in a sewing factory in Winnipeg, making jeans. We got 35¢ an hour for an eight-hour day.

We worked five days a week in the factory, and on Saturdays I cleaned houses. We were able to save most of our factory money, and the $4 I made on Saturdays kept the two of us for a week. We bought milk and bread and vegetables and soup bones. We made plenty of soup. Sunday was the only day we had meat.

You have to remember that we had lived for years on a similar diet as refugees in Europe, so it wasn't the hardship for us that it would have been for other people. At the end of a year, we had saved $1,000 and some distant relatives in the Winkler area lent us another $1,000 to put a deposit on a two-storey house on Notre Dame, here in Winnipeg. That house cost $6,000 in 1951, and my mother sold it two years ago for $26,000!

Those Winkler relatives were so kind to us. They met us when we arrived, and they kept my younger sister with them in the country until we had that house.

I got married after I'd worked in that factory for a year. A Mennonite friend introduced me to her cousin. He had eleven brothers and sisters. They came in the 1920s, when he was one year old. His family made all the wedding arrangements, and it was such a big wedding. There were over two hundred people there. It was so good to be part of a big family. My father died in Siberia, and my brother died in a prison camp in Russia. There were only my mother, my young sister and me left, to come to Canada. *Mennonite immigrant.*

"Language was our biggest problem."

After our year was up, the railway gave us a free pass to anywhere in Canada. Most guys went to Toronto, but I came to Hamilton. I had a friend there. After six weeks, I got a job at Stelco, a labourer's job in the foundry. "Just give me a job," I said. I could speak only a little bit of English.

Language was our biggest problem, and sometimes people tried to cheat us. My friend and I, we rented a room, and later we found out the landlady was charging us double. The two of us were sleeping in the same room, in the same single bed, but on different shifts. It took us a month to figure out what she was doing.

Four years later, after I was married, I contracted tuberculosis, and for eighteen months I was off work, in the sanatorium. That was a very hard time for my wife, living on welfare, $80 a month, with two little boys to keep, and $50 of it going on rent. During that time in the sanatorium, I decided to take some courses to better myself. I studied accountancy, and after I was well enough to go back to Stelco, I wrote the exams at night school, in English. So I went to the personnel office, and asked for a different job, in accounts. But the same guy who'd interviewed me all those years before pulls my file out and says, "Ah — broken English. There's no job for you in accounting, Ivan, you can't speak good enough English."

I should have quit, I know, but you're afraid to lose a job after you've been sick, when you have two kids, a house and a mortgage. So I stayed with Stelco, and I got an easier job in shipping. I've done well there, but I've never been able to use my accounting course. *Slovenian immigrant.*

Steel manufacture, Hamilton. In 1952, the average wage for steelworkers was $1.41 an hour for labourers, $1.71 for ladlemen and $2.79 for rollers.

No Canadian Licence

At the Embassy in Copenhagen, they told me I'd have no trouble getting work as an electrician, but they forgot to tell me that I needed a Canadian licence. I found that out when I got to Ottawa, and it took time to get one. So I went to a construction site, looking for work. I went every morning at 7:00 a.m., and someone would come out of the office and pick, "you — you — and you." One day he picked me. I'd never done hard work in my life before.

It was so hot that summer, and they put a bucket of ice water for us to drink, all of us from the same bucket. I was horrified, and I wouldn't touch it at first. But after two days, I was drinking from it along with the rest.

It took me several months to find work in my own field. Then I worked for $1.50 a hour. But my wife took in sewing, and we found that five people could live on $18 a week, if they were careful. *Danish immigrant.*

"My first break."

In 1952, I was eighteen, and I'd already had three years apprenticeship as a watchmaker in Scotland. We'd gone to Glasgow as refugees after the war, but my mother couldn't stand the climate there. So we came to Canada in February 1952, and I walked the streets of Toronto for four months. There was just nothing to do.

The priest from our church was very outgoing, and he gave me $50 to help keep my mother. And in the end, I got a job in an instrument factory, and that was my first break. *Polish immigrant.*

Unemployed immigrants demonstrate in Toronto, 1952. In February that year, two hundred men, staying at the immigration hostel at St.-Paul-l'Ermite, Quebec, went on a brief hunger strike because of the lack of jobs and the consequent delay in bringing their wives and children to Canada, from refugee camps in Germany.

Yonge Street subway construction, Toronto, 1950.

On the Flimsiest Promise

We felt that Germany had no future after the war, and we came to Canada on the flimsiest promise. My husband wrote to all the provincial medical colleges, and the only one to answer was Alberta. They said there *might* be an opening for an intern in Edmonton. Just in case there wasn't, Henry took a course as an electric welder. He was even prepared to work in a mine, but the immigration people said he was too tall and too old. Henry was a skin specialist and he was forty-five years old.

When we got to Edmonton, we had a terrible experience. The Secretary of the Alberta College told Henry the best thing that could have happened after the war was if they had shot every German left alive. We expected the worst, but in the end we were surprised and delighted. Henry was hired as an intern at the University hospital, in spite of the Secretary. But the doctor in charge advised Henry that, if politics came up in conversation, he shouldn't join in. It was too early to talk about the war, he said.

We couldn't speak much English, but Henry had learned the basics as a prisoner of war in the United States. We quite deliberately concentrated on speaking English at home. There was a Dutch intern at the hospital, and Henry noticed his English was all gone after he'd been home for a weekend. Henry had to take his exams in English, and he was forty-five, but it never occurred to him he could fail.

Life was difficult until he passed. Interns got paid $40 a month, and we had two little girls, aged one and a half and two and a half. We lived in a small basement apartment, and I took a job as a maid at a sanatorium, for $143 a month. It was so hard on the children, they cried and cried when I took them to the babysitter every day. How can you explain to two little tykes that it's only for one year? In Germany, we'd had a comfortable life, and my friends wrote to me, "How can you work as a maid, and live in a cellar, when you're a doctor's wife?" But it was all I could do, with such a limited command of the language.

Those hospital doctors were wonderful people. The doctor in charge insisted on lending us $50 a month, and another doctor did the same. We lived off their kindness until Henry passed his exams, and then he went to a small town for a few years, as a general practitioner. He loved it. *German immigrant.*

No Self-pity

I'd studied architecture in Hungary, and I hoped to get taken on by a firm in Montreal. But first, I needed a haircut to make me look presentable. In Europe, good hotels have good barbers, so I went down to the Windsor Hotel. In Europe, you don't shave, the barber does it, so I asked for a shave, and I even had my moustache singed. That barber did a wonderful job — but it cost me $10, and that was a worrying experience. It was the equivalent of one week's pension in a small hotel in Austria, where we'd been living.

I looked in the Montreal phone book to find the Architects' Association address, and then I went down and asked the lady on the desk how to get a job. The Association has always been very self-protective, but then it was more so than ever. She said, "Here you're not an architect. At best, you're a draftsman. Go and look in the yellow pages."

Rue Ste-Catherine, Montreal, 1952.

Never Doubted Canada

I wrote to the Association of Professional Engineers in Ontario, asking about jobs, but they wouldn't consider you, unless you actually came to Canada. So you had to take a chance. It was an attempt at a closed shop, but I knew they didn't have enough engineers, so I came anyway, in 1953.

I first got the idea about coming to Canada in an Exmouth pub, in 1951. I met this Canadian who'd been a "dollar-a-year" man in the war years. He was a big realtor, and said he'd give me a hand if I came over. I'd been telling him about the high taxes in England, and bemoaning the Labour government's "cradle-to-the-grave" socialism and the restrictions on private enterprise.

When I got to Toronto, he gave me a base, an office to phone from and to use as an address. He told me about the progressive municipalities, and I phoned around to Scarborough, North York and Etobicoke. I phoned Etobicoke last because I couldn't pronounce it, but that was where I got offered a job. It wasn't a very good job, because I hadn't got my papers yet as an Ontario engineer.

Etobicoke was expanding terribly fast. A thousand people a day were coming in there, and the engineering department couldn't cope. A friend and I were responsible for checking engineering drawings, and we began to think that we could do better ourselves. So we set up as consulting engineers in 1955. Our office was an apartment over a small store, in the beginning.

Toronto was growing fast, and we grew with it. There were several times when we got worried, but I never doubted that Canada was the better place to live. *English immigrant.*

Most of the architects' offices seemed to be on St. Catharines West, so I made a list, in order, and I decided to start at Guy, with the farthest number, and work my way back. I had some good chats along the way, but no jobs, until I went into a very old firm, and the boss came out of his office, by chance, just when his secretary was trying to send me away. He listened to me, and he hired me as a draftsman. I was to come back on November 1, for the unheard-of salary of $200 a month. That was four months' salary for a school principal in Austria.

It wasn't always easy. I lost that job after a while, because the firm had no more work for me, and I had to go looking again. But I could speak good English, and my first principle was, always, that I wasn't going to sit and mope and be miserable with a group of Hungarians. *Hungarian immigrant.*

A Yen for Travel

If I'd known what I found out when I arrived here in 1951, to work for Avro, I'd have come out four years earlier. But in 1947, when I graduated in engineering from Edinburgh University, I was called up to do my National Service. [two years compulsory service in the British Armed Forces]. I could have missed that by coming to Canada. But I did it, and when I finished I got an ex-serviceman's grant to go to an aeronautical college, at Cranfield.

In 1950, I wrote off to various companies looking for work, and I got interviewed by Avro, in London. They offered me the princely sum of $3,000 to start, in Toronto, and that was almost twice what anybody in England offered me. So I decided to come to Canada. I had a yen for travel, and emigration had been in my mind for a long time. In Scotland, the only engineering jobs available were in shipbuilding, so I knew I'd have to leave home, anyway.

Five or six people from our year at Cranfield ended up in Canada, but this was just before the big advertising campaign, which brought lots of British engineers to work in the aircraft industry. Six months after I came, these companies were paying people's fares to get them over here, but I missed that opportunity. I came over on the *Ascania*, and I paid my own way.

I went to work for Avro Engines, the forerunner of Orenda. They were building engines for the CF 100 and the Sabre jet, and they had started working on the Iroquois, which was intended for the Avro Arrow. There was a lot of creativity at Avro, but during the two years I was there, there seemed to be a crisis every three months, as government contracts ran out. The whole future of the place depended on defence contracts and the government's whim, and I didn't trust the government.

I looked around for something else, and I got a job with Atomic Energy of Canada, at Chalk River. I was fascinated by nuclear energy. There were very few people with any experience in the nuclear field, so they took people from different backgrounds. When I joined, there were several of us from the aircraft engine business, and some chaps from the automobile industry.

I was married by the time I took this job. My fiancée was finishing her nursing training in England, when I came to Canada, so for the first nine months, I batched it with another fellow. Three days after she arrived, we got married. Her uncle in Toronto, whom she'd never seen, met her at four o'clock and gave her away at five. We rented a place in Toronto for a while, but going to Chalk River meant that we got a house of our own. It would have taken two more years in Toronto to save up for the down payment on a house there.

The Atomic Energy plant was at Chalk River, but we lived in Deep River, a beautiful spot right on the Ottawa River. There were under three thousand people living there, and 30% or 40% of them were British immigrants. The average age was thirty when we got there, and Deep River had the highest birthrate of any town in Canada then. Two of our five children were born there. *Scottish immigrant.*

Dam construction, Consolidated Mining and Smelting Co. power development on Pend d'Oreille River, near Trail, British Columbia, June 1952.

Construction Tragedy

We were working on a coffer dam on the Nechako River, and the water from the river went through this tunnel, which they'd blasted through the mountain. At the entrance to the tunnel, ice had formed, and the labour gang foreman said, "You put on your boots and rope yourselves to that tree, and then get out to break the ice."

He gave us special boots with nails in the soles, but one of the workers didn't put them on. He was one of the immigrants who'd come after the war, and his English was poor. This man didn't put the special boots on, and when he went down to the ice, he fell into the water. He was dragged through the tunnel, and when they found his body, it was soft all over, like a sponge. There were no bones left in it. He was one of the new fellows, Ukrainian I think, and there was a big row, big trouble about this accident. *Polish immigrant, British Columbia.*

"You came to make your dollar . . . ."

Going to Kitimat was one of the great adventures of my life, and we came into it with a lot of enthusiasm. In 1953, it was a man's world, an immigrant's world. There was quite a publicity campaign about it in Germany, and my father came to work on the docks. He'd been in the merchant marine.

Father went ahead, and my brother and I — we were just teenagers — we followed in August, by ourselves. We sailed from Bremerhaven, on the *Arosa Star*, and it was a terrible tub, but we couldn't have cared less. Everything was new, different, exciting.

Postwar Germany was stifling in many ways. Everywhere was so crowded. We always seemed to be queuing up for things, to be brushing against people, or past people. I was seventeen, and at that age in Germany, I would have been hitting the books, trying to get into university. I came from a typical bourgeois environment, from a city rich in tradition. Here, I went to high school in a Quonset hut, and you did Grade 13 by correspondence. There were very few kids, to start with.

You had to be pretty self-sufficient to appreciate Kitimat in 1953. There were no roads, no pavement, and you walked around in gumboots and heavy jackets, which you bought at the Hudson's Bay store. We were a family, but we were the exception. Most of the population were bachelors, and a lot of them lived on one of the old sternwheelers, the *Delta King*, which the company moored in the Kitimat channel and turned into a bunkhouse. There were no girls around, to start with, and the drinking and gambling were fantastic. Things began to change, though, in 1954,

The *Delta King*, moored in the Kitimat channel, was used as a bunkhouse for Alcan workers.

when the families came in.

It was such a cosmopolitan community. Kitimat and Kemano were like the world in miniature. The emphasis was on making money — you came to make your dollar, and then you left. The turnover was two or three years among my German friends. Unskilled workers went into filthy jobs, but they were well paid, and they could work overtime. And some of the ones who left came back again. They missed the mountains and the outdoor life. I left to go to university, but my father stayed on there until he retired, seventeen years after he arrived. *German immigrant.*

Beaverlodge, Saskatchewan, Eldorado Mining and Refining Co.

A Chance Meeting

I went to the Northwest Territories, to the Thompson River area, prospecting for uranium. That part of the country is real isolated. There's no settlement, no planes flying around, and you feel sort of lonely, and yet it's exciting being in a place like that. Our base of operations was Uranium City, and I saw a lot of the north country that year.

We spent six weeks prospecting on one trip, and finally we ran out of grub. We had no trouble catching fish, mostly jackfish. But fish, whether you boil it or fry it or smoke it, doesn't taste very good without salt, even when you're hungry. We ate rabbits and berries too, and I was surprised at how you can get by without much in the bush. But I still wish we'd had some salt.

One time, I was staking claims, and I came to the end of the line. I lifted my head up and there was a bear, maybe three or four feet away. We both got startled you know. I lifted my axe, but my hand was shaky. He stood up on his hind legs, and I knew he was scared too. We looked at each other for a second or two . . . to me it felt like a couple of hours . . . and then he took off one way, and I took off the other. When I ran out of breath, I stopped and looked back, and the bear stopped and looked back at me. After that, we continued running away from one another. *Polish immigrant.*

With an Open Mind

Drilling operations, Taber, Alberta.

Sure, it was different from what I was used to. But you come to a new country, and what you used to have, what you used to be, those are things of the past. This is now your home, and you live by the rules.

You have to be thankful you've got a job. I started out in the Leduc oilfields, southwest of Edmonton, stringing barbed wire around land which the company leased from the farmers. In those days, the beer parlour in the Devon Hotel was the local field office. I earned 80¢ an hour, working in temperatures of 28 or 30 degrees below zero [fahrenheit], and it was cold, but I could laugh it off. It wasn't a bad job.

A month later, I was a chainman, and I kept moving on. My biggest asset was my English. I became an instrument man, I got into drafting, I worked in a gas compressor, and I got to be a block foreman for Mobil, in charge of maintenance crews in Drayton Valley. I also served beer in a tavern in my spare time!

The main thing was, I came with an open mind. I was accepted by people, I made friends, I've always been in good company here. *Danish immigrant.*

VIII Impressions

Vancouver, 1940s.

On a Huge Scale

We got on the train at Halifax, and I couldn't believe the size of the wheels on the locomotive. European trains were like toys, by comparison. Everything seemed to be on a huge scale — the train, the meals we were served, even the candies, or sweets, as we called them. And that went for the country itself — hundreds of miles of prairie, huge mountains and rivers, endless forests and bush. *Scottish immigrant.*

Words You Mustn't Say

My sister wrote to me about words I must not say or use in Canada, because they meant something quite different here. Above all, I mustn't ask the train porter to "knock me up" in the morning, and I did remember that. But I still made lots of mistakes, like the time I horrified the man at the fish counter by asking for "a nice piece of tail." I meant salmon, of course.

It was ages before I learned to say "Hi!" to people instead of "Hello, how are you?" Whenever I tried to say "Hi!" it was as if something stuck in my throat.

Housekeeping was so easy, I couldn't get over it — the washer and dryer, the electric floor polisher, the exhaust fan over the stove, the constant hot water. It bothered me, after wartime Britain, where we were so conscious of conserving everything, only lighting the boiler before we had a bath, only using the car for necessities. Here, people got into a car to go to the corner store, and it bothered me. *Scottish immigrant.*

En route to Vancouver, 1949.

New Ways were Frightening

My husband was ill with bronchitis, and I wanted to buy some liquor, to make gluhwein, to warm him. But where to buy it? My neighbour said, "There is a special store for liquor, and you must write down your name and address on a piece of paper, and give it to the man." Well, I was too frightened to go. I thought, if I must say who I am, and where I live to buy this, then there is something wrong. In the end, my kind neighbour went to the liquor store for me.

Does this sound crazy to you? The things that happened to me in Europe made me afraid like that. *Slovenian immigrant, Sudbury.*

German immigrants, Montreal.

"Three rooms to Ourselves!"

We searched and searched for an apartment in Montreal, and at last we found one, in a three-storey walk-up. Imagine! Three rooms to ourselves! It cost $65 a month. Another immigrant had been living there, and we only got it on condition that we bought his furniture. We were so eager, we agreed at once. But about four weeks later, Eatons or Simpsons came round to repossess everything. Apparently, this man had not kept up his payments. As immigrants, this was the kind of trap you could fall into.

A space-heater sat in the middle of the hall, and there was an oil drum on the balcony, outside the kitchen door. My little sister played out there, and one day she fell backwards, down the iron stairs outside. We didn't know the neighbours. We kept very much to ourselves, but everybody rushed around. They called a doctor, an ambulance. That changed our approach to people.

I was nine, and I was left at home a lot to look after the other kids. In Germany, there were no such things as babysitters. I'd be told to take my little sister out in the stroller, and I hated it. I was afraid people would speak to me, and I wouldn't understand. One day, somebody did say something, and I just said, "Deutsch." She didn't know what I meant. She thought I'd said, "Dutch." It's odd, but it really bothered me. It was summer, and I hadn't started to learn English at school. *German immigrant.*

Fantastic Community Spirit

There was a fantastic housing shortage in Fredericton, when we arrived in 1948. The Veterans and their families had gobbled up all the space. But the university had promised my husband there would be accommodation, and they told us we would be living in Alexander College.

I imagined an old, ivy-covered building, New England-style, but the college was an old army camp, put up on the Exhibition grounds. To me, it looked very like a concentration camp. Our unit had two small rooms and a kitchen, and there were army chairs and tables and beds with grey army blankets. We had to share a bathroom with another family. For three days I sat on the bed and refused to unpack. After the war, after the last few years in Czechoslovakia, I felt the world would never return to normal.

A few weeks passed, and I found there was a fantastic community spirit among the families living in that place. They made the army huts look as much like home as they could. People put flowerpots out on the steps, and somebody called Phyllis had this sporting British attitude. She took me to buy four orange crates, and she showed me how to make bookshelves out of them.

If we'd gone to Montreal or Toronto, we would have become part of the Czech communities there. But we were the second Europeans to arrive in Fredericton after the war, and we were very conspicuous. I remember walking down Queen Street, talking to my young son, and I noticed people listening. Eventually, a lady stopped us and asked, ''What language are you speaking? Czech? Oh, where's that? How interesting! Are you visiting?'' *Czech immigrant.*

Alexander College, University of New Brunswick, provided classroom space and living quarters in former military barracks on the grounds of the Fredericton Exhibition.

British warbrides and their families, evicted from disused military buildings on St. Helen's Island, Montreal, where they had lived as squatters, 1947.

A Homeless Immigrant

Dear Sir:

As an Irish immigrant I would like to point out a few things in this country which I do not think is justice to a British subject.

First is this. Why are English-speaking British subjects brushed aside to allow Germans, Poles and Dutch, etc. to take jobs out of our hands?

I came out here a year ago and have a wife and three children back in Ireland and am unable to get them out here because I cannot get a place for them to live.

I went to see about a job where a house was supplied and was told that I could not have the job because there was a Dutch family coming for it, but they had not left Holland yet.

Well, I am an ex-service man serving from 1940 to 1946. I fought with the Inniskillin Fusiliers from North Africa, Sicily, Italy and right through Austria.

I left home to come out here for a decent job and a place to bring my family up, and all I find is a land of promise and the people I fought taking the best of jobs from under my nose and bringing their families with them.

I feel sometimes that we are not wanted in Canada but you don't walk home from here.

T. Downey, Ottawa.

Letter to the Ottawa Citizen, *May 1952.*

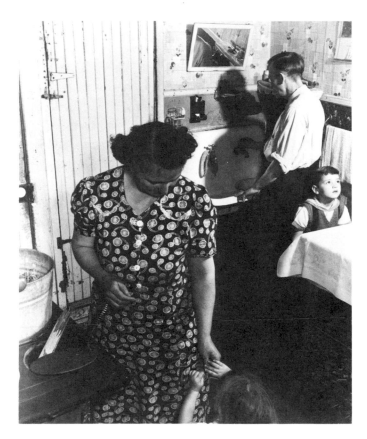

Cabbagetown, Toronto, 1949.

A Wonderful Landlady

Mrs. Thompson, our landlady, was a widow and an absolute dear. She came from England, and she kept the house like an English cottage, with roses all round. She must have weighed 200 pounds, and she got up at five o'clock every morning to shovel coal into the furnace.

We paid her $12 a week for a kitchen, a bathroom, one bedroom and a living room, and food for the two of us cost $15. *English immigrant, Toronto.*

Unscrupulous Operators

It was very difficult for a family with children to rent accommodation in Toronto after the war, and many immigrants were forced into buying property. Sometimes they were the victims of unscrupulous operators.

One man came to us with a complaint that he had bought a house, but when he took possession, he found it had been completely stripped of everything, from door knobs, to taps, to light fixtures. When I checked with the seller, I discovered that the conditions were all included in the document he'd signed, but in very small print. His English being what it was, he had not bothered to try to read the fine print.

We finally did manage to get his deposit back, but it wasn't the easiest task in the world. *Social worker, Toronto.*

Regent Park rental housing development, Toronto, 1949.

Discovering the Supermarket

Mother and I went shopping for the first time in a supermarket, and we loaded a cart right up to the top. All that sugar and butter and meat and eggs — she'd never seen so much all together. When we got to the cash, we couldn't pay for it all. We had to leave some of it behind. I couldn't get over how clean everything was, so sanitary, so gleaming. The meat was all wrapped in refrigerated cases, whereas in Britain, you could see the blue-bottles [flies] settling on the meat in the butcher's window. *Scottish immigrant.*

Part of Your Culture

Sauerkraut we could get from Lunenberg, and some smoked meats from a little Jewish delicatessen. Some of us started smoking our own meat and fish, and making our own cheeses.

Food is so important, a part of your culture. Mainly we missed the dark rye bread. We eastern Europeans craved it, and we couldn't make it because we couldn't buy the flour. And we Latvians couldn't bake our special bread for Christmas, because you need poppy seeds, and nobody knew what those were, in Halifax. People would say, "You mean popcorn." *Latvian immigrant, Dartmouth.*

Plain Food

All the bread was white and sliced, and there were just three kinds of cheese at the store — cheddar, Kraft slices and the kind of cheese you spread. After France, it was not very appealing. But I could live on $10 a week — $5 for food and $5 for a room. *French immigrant, Vancouver.*

Kept Our Names

The school principal in Kingston wanted us to change our names. He thought I should be called Sylvia, and my sister should be Elizabeth. Things would be easier for us, he said. We'd be accepted faster by the other kids who had trouble pronouncing our names.

We couldn't see that changing our names would make us any different from what we were — immigrant kids from a refugee camp. And our names were just about the only things we'd brought with us. *East German immigrant.*

"It was my pride . . . ."

I went into Grade 12 in Sudbury, when we arrived, and for three weeks I wore the same outfit. What a humiliation! Each night, I would wash and dry it. A girl in the class offered me some of her clothes, but I said, "No thank you." It was my pride; I was stupid then.

But I got this babysitting job, and after three weeks, I bought myself a new blouse. When I wore it to school the next day, the whole class all broke out into applause. *Croatian immigrant.*

"Being different mattered so much."

I was twelve and my sister was thirteen when we came to Ottawa. The local principal wouldn't take both of us at the same school. He said, "You'll never learn English, if you can see each other in recess. We'll have to separate you." That made things harder than they might have been.

My teacher really tried to teach me English, but she used these little kids' books. It made me feel a fool, reading out, "This is a dog. Here is a cat." I wanted to tell her, but I couldn't. There weren't any books then to teach older kids English.

I felt like a freak, I was so different from the other kids. We'd been brought up to be so polite — we curtsied to say "hello" to adults, and we always stood up when the teacher came in. And I wore the wrong clothes to school. In Denmark, you wore slacks and jeans, but in Ottawa I was the only girl who did. Being different mattered so much. I dreaded lunchtime, because my mother made me these open-faced sandwiches, and you had to eat them with a knife and fork. Nobody else had food like that, and I ate as fast as I could, and then I'd rush out, with indigestion. *Danish immigrant.*

Immigrant children, Ottawa, 1950s.

"... them and me against the world."

I was just nineteen when I started teaching. I'd been in Canada a year, and I took a six-week summer course to qualify. Later, I had to go to teachers' college, but this was the "baby-boom," and you had your choice of schools in southern Ontario. I chose St. Catharines, because I had this romantic concept — it was near Niagara Falls.

The school was very mixed. It was in an immigrant district, predominantly Italian and Slovak, with some Dutch too. The principal was a nun. Those European parents had such trusting faith in the teacher as authority. They believed the teacher was there to discipline children.

I felt a great affinity for those kids, and they identified with me. They felt foreign, and my name was foreign. I came from Guyana, British Guyana it was then, and my parents were Portuguese and Spanish. I lived in the immigrant district, and my apartment became a focal point for the kids. They came at night, for coaching and for companionship. It was them and me against the world, against the principal, against Canada.

They saw themselves as different, apart. The older kids got sent into Grade 1 with the little ones, to learn English, and that was humiliating. The word "DP" was thrown around in the playground, by kids from the very same backgrounds, except these were second generation kids. They felt they belonged here. *Guyanese immigrant.*

German Baptists (Volksdeutsch) at prayer in sugar beet field near Lethbridge, Alberta.

"The missing pieces ..."

We lost something terribly dear, terribly important, when we had to flee from our country, and it was this loss that held our community together. Everything centered around our Church. It sustained us and it satisfied the missing pieces in our lives.

There was the dear, familiar service, and a priest who spoke our own language and advised us on so many things. He helped us find a place to live, and he helped my husband to get a job. You can't begin to understand the comfort and the support we received unless you came here as a refugee, with no money and no English and no friends. *Slovenian immigrant, Ontario.*

Church social group, 1940s.

"Church was a club . . ."

On Monday, the teacher always asked, "Who went to Sunday school?" and if you hadn't, she looked horrified and asked, "Why not?"

Everything was so holy on Sunday. You couldn't hang out your washing, you couldn't do anything except go to Church. The United

Church was a club, really, as much as a religious place. My parents were told, "That's where you'll make your contacts, and get your business," and for the first few years we all went. In Denmark we were middle class, but here we were nothing, to start with. *Danish immigrant, Ottawa.*

Street Car Talk

To the Editor of the *Star:*

Sir: Last night I got on a street car feeling fine, but believe me, I certainly had a headache when I got off. Directly behind me sat a foreign-speaking couple, talking so loud that you couldn't possibly carry on a conversation with anyone sitting next to you. When this couple got off they spoke good English to the motorman. Why, when they are able to speak English, and, I presume, are making Canada their home, do they not speak the language of this country, at least when out in public? They would certainly get more respect from Canadian citizens than the glares they were getting last night. This is only one of many times I have had to listen to this sort of thing.

> *(signed) K.O.*
> *Toronto* Star, *April 28, 1953.*

Likes Own Language

To the Editor of the *Star:*

Sir: I think no matter what language you speak, if you speak too loudly that is not polite. But K.O. objected not to the loudness but to a foreign language being spoken in public. In what way does he think the English language superior to any other? For me my native language is most beautiful. So why should I not speak it — because K.O. and others like him do not understand it? I think it is a great thing to know several languages. You have to be pretty smart to learn them. As to getting respect from Canadian citizens, I do not think speaking English in public plays any part in this. At any rate, why should I strive to gain the respect of people who are so prejudiced they bridle when they hear a foreign language spoken?

> *(signed) D.H.*
> *Toronto* Star, *May 1, 1953.*

Wants English in Public

To the Editor of the *Star:*

Sir: Having a slight knowledge of both the French and German languages, I feel that they should not be displayed in public in Canada — especially where the English language is predominant.

> *(signed) Courteous*
> *Toronto* Star, *May 4, 1953.*

University Avenue, Toronto, 1950.

Fish and Fog

No one could tell us anything about Newfoundland at Canada House, in London, where
we were living as refugees. 1948 was the year
before Confederation. "There's fish and fog,"
they said, and, "Do take a long dress, because
they have lots of parties in Newfoundland." It was
incredible what they didn't tell us. They should
have said, "Bring anything, everything you have
in the way of furniture."

The university paid our way. The salary was
only $3,000, and it was hard for them to get people
to stay. But as refugees we jumped at the chance.
We were the first outsiders to "come from
aways," apart from some mainlanders, and we
were a great attraction. We came over Christmas,
on a Furness Withy boat from Liverpool, and St.
John's looked like fairyland as we came into the
harbour. There were Christmas trees all lit up on
the hill, and the dirt was all covered by snow, with
all those gaily painted wooden houses standing out
against the white. And the head of the department
was standing waiting for us on the dock.

People were so nice to us. The second day, we
went walking. It was Sunday morning, and a complete stranger said, "You look new — would you
like Sunday dinner?" *Austrian refugee.*

Germans in Newfoundland

I came to Newfoundland to work in one of Joey
Smallwood's new industries, and I wondered how
Newfoundlanders would feel about Germans. It
was so soon after the war, and I'd been in the German air force.

We were not much liked at first, my wife and
me, but we were so sensitive to things people said,

St. John's, Newfoundland, mid-1940s.

and sometimes there were misunderstandings.
One time I had a terrible cold, and I kept sneezing
at work. After a while, the man I worked with got
mad and said, "Hey! Keep your bloody germs
away from me!" But what I thought he said was,
"Keep those bloody Germans away from me!"
And I got fighting mad. My English was good, but
it wasn't perfect, and sometimes I wasn't sure
what people meant.

Newfoundlanders could be really strange. Getting a place to live was so difficult when we
arrived, and for a time we lived in this small flat,
my wife and me and the baby. Then somebody
offered to rent us his house for a year. But it was in
a Veterans' Housing development, and there was
a great fuss because we were Germans. Then the
owner said to his neighbours, "Listen, it's alright,
he's a war veteran." And after that it was okay —
honest! We got along fine. That's Newfoundland
for you. *German immigrant.*

Money to be Made

People were so worn down by austerity after the war, and everyone in Britain was talking about going *somewhere* — Canada? Australia? New Zealand? Kenya? the Rhodesias? South Africa? The idea that Canada was big and open, with cities to build and money to be made, was an all-pervasive thing. I would like to say that money wasn't uppermost in my mind, but it wouldn't be entirely true.

We came for material reasons, yet we had trouble adapting to a place where people talked about money all the time. My wife was told that joining a church would be very good for my career as an architect, and the one I should join was the Anglican Church down the road, because there was lots of money there. The whole thing stuck in my gullet, and I never went near the place.

We missed the quality of things we'd taken for granted in England — music, china, woollen clothing. *English immigrant.*

Unspoken Friction

I felt a complete and total stranger for years. There was always this unspoken friction. Canadians felt superior to us, because of the way we talked, the way we dressed, the things we ate. And we felt superior to them. We thought our education, our outlook so much broader, so much more sophisticated. Perhaps it was a mistake on both sides. They were very provincial and narrow-minded, and we were more limited than we realised. We knew European life and literature, but we didn't know much about North America. *Hungarian immigrant.*

''Father was strict about English . . .''

Father was so strict about English that even at home, we were not allowed to say anything in Chinese. If we wanted to talk to Mother, we did it through Father, who translated. Mother understood we had to learn and that was all there was to it. But she was very lonely.

My father's brothers had Caucasian wives, so they were a lost cause for my mother. They just sat and smiled at each other, but they didn't say a word. She stayed in the house all winter, and then, in the spring, we were out shopping and she saw this old Chinese woman on the street. Mother charged up and introduced herself. I was so embarrassed because she did it all in Chinese, but she felt so cooped up. *Chinese immigrant, Vancouver.*

Culture Shock

Edmonton was so cold. That was shocking. We arrived at the end of January. I learned to go from one store to the next, and then the next. But that first night in the hotel, my husband touched me and I got an electric shock and I was scared.

There were other Japanese people in Edmonton, and they got together and ordered Japanese food from Vancouver. I was pleased. I expected to do without it. But these Japanese people seemed strange at first, because I didn't know the Canadian customs. Very often my husband would tell jokes and I wouldn't understand, and by the time he explained, it wasn't funny anymore. *Japanese immigrant.*

So Many Jews

My sponsor found me work on a farm in the Kingston area. One weekend, a friend drove me to Montreal, to see the big city, and I remember standing and staring outside the YMHA. There were Jews everywhere! I had ceased to believe that Jews existed in large groups anywhere anymore — and there were so many of them here. *Polish Jew, Auschwitz survivor.*

Self-conscious about Identity

I was self-conscious about being German, maybe because we lived in a very Jewish neighbourhood in Montreal, off Decarie. My parents' friends were mostly German immigrants like themselves, and in our household the grown-ups' language was German, although the children's language was English.

When I was a teenager, a friend of the family gave me this beautiful embroidered peasant blouse, and I refused to wear it. No one else at school wore things like that, and it made me feel German when I wanted so badly to be Canadian.

Then *The Sound of Music* came out, and everybody wanted those peasant blouses. *German immigrant.*

French among the French Canadians

The majority of Montrealers spoke French but, alas, you quickly discovered that ignorance of English diminished your chances of finding work. You could speak French in Montreal, but you worked in English. The Anglo-Saxons held all the economic levers in their hands.

It was difficult for someone from France to feel part of Quebec in the 1950s. French Canadians seemed older as a society than we did, in one sense, and yet newer in another. They were tied to their past by traditions and folklore and religion, and yet they had adopted an American standard of living which masked their unique character. *French immigrant, who returned to France.*

"Refugee Boulevard," Fletcher's Field, Montreal, outside Jewish Immigrant Aid Services office, 1949.

"Toronto the Good"

It was very much "Toronto the Good" in those days. I was living by myself in a single room, and there were no pubs or Saturday night "hops" where I could meet people and have a good time, like I did in England.

The only way I could hope to meet eligible girls was through joining a church group of one kind or another. When I left the U.K., religion wasn't a major part of my life, but in Toronto it was very important. *English immigrant.*

Boys kept at Home

Our social life revolved around the church, and the church didn't have dances. The Y put on some dances for immigrants, but Father was not in favour of us going. You couldn't trust strangers, he said. He meant, particularly, strange women.

Dutch parents really controlled their children, and the pressure was always on us to stay home. We were a large family, mainly boys, and you didn't do *anything* with girls! I was twenty-one before I was allowed to go out to a dance. Can you believe that? *Dutch immigrant, Fredericton.*

Just a Little Boy

We went to Lac Philippe, in the summer, and my little boy ran around on the beach with no clothes on. And people said, "Quick! Get him dressed, or the police will come!"

He was just a little boy, aged four. *Danish immigrant.*

The Rules of the Game

Dating girls, the kind I wanted to go out with, was very difficult. It wasn't just my accent that sounded different, I really *was* different, because the rules of the game were different where I came from. We were much more open and straightforward about showing how we appreciated women.

In Montreal, and again in Windsor, I frightened off many of the girls I approached by being so direct, so enthusiastic. And even after I toned down my approach, I found many girls were afraid of marrying someone from central Europe. We were supposed to be romantic and passionate — but great womanizers, basically unreliable. *Hungarian immigrant.*

Peculiar Social Occasions

Dear H.,

We were invited this week to a ball held by the Chamber of Commerce. Canadian social occasions of this kind are rather peculiar, as they are very informal. They begin at 9:00 p.m., and by 10:00 p.m. most people have arrived. Each gentleman has brought a lady, as it is impossible for a single man to find a partner there. You buy tickets ahead of time — they are given to the waiter in exchange for drinks. Each man dances only with his lady, and by midnight half the crowd has left. In any case, everything is shut down by 1:00 a.m., so the dance has lasted no longer than three hours! *German immigrant, Montreal, writing to a friend in Germany, October 1953.*

"Rum and Whiskey!"

Going out to a club to dance in Halifax was so different from Germany. There was nothing club-like about it. The men all brought their own bottles along and hid them under the table. The stuff they drank! All that rum and whiskey! You wouldn't believe it.

I'd say to the man who brought me, "Come on, you've had enough," and he'd say, "I can't feel anything yet." I think they went there just to get stoned. *German immigrant.*

Saturday Night Dances

To get a drink of rum in Edmonton in 1951, you had to buy a bottle in a liquor store. There were no cocktail lounges. In 1953, they got "ladies and escorts" bars, but you couldn't go in there unless you had a woman with you already, and that could be quite a problem for a single man, come into town from the oilfields looking for some female company. Outside the city, though, it was different. The place to go was St. Albert, to the old Bruin Hotel, where they didn't care about segregating the men and the women.

Drinking was illegal in Edmonton dance halls like the Trocadero and the Rainbow, but there were tables with little ledges underneath, and that's where you hid your mickey. You bought some ginger ale at the dance hall and you mixed your own drinks. In the smaller towns there were Saturday night dances where you paid 50¢ to get in, and you got your hand stamped to prove it. The drinking took place in the cars outside; there were no tables or chairs round the dance floor. But all the farmers' daughters from round about came, and some Indian girls too. The local band played, and you yahooed and did your thing. *Danish immigrant.*

A Lonely Bachelor

After I left the farm, I got a job as a painter in Regina. If you spoke German, you could get by in Regina in 1952. There were so many older immigrants, and people like me who'd been in the camps. When I rode to work on the bus early in the morning, everybody spoke German, except maybe the driver.

I was in Regina one and a half years before I met anyone else who'd come from Czechoslovakia. Being single, and not speaking much English and living in a rented room, I was very lonely. I had no idea how much I would miss my own people, or even the people I lived with in the refugee camp.

There were so few places to meet people, particularly women. Women were not allowed in beer parlours, and Regina didn't have cocktail lounges in those days. On Sundays, when I had the whole day off, there were no movies, and no restaurants open. In summer, I would go for walks in Wascana Park, but in winter there was nowhere to go.

It was a hard time for me. I knew there was no way to go home. Somehow, you have to live, to go ahead. *Czech immigrant.*

Regina, mid-1940s.

German family, Montreal, mid-1950s.

The Self-made Man

We have become the kind of Canadians who are like converted Catholics — super-super nationalists. One thing that matters a great deal in Europe doesn't matter here: who your father was, what he did, where you came from. Social status is not static here as it was in Germany. Here is the place for the self-made man. Here, new money doesn't smell. Maybe it's valued too much as motivation, but if you don't want to join in the race, you are free to opt out. Here, you can live the life you want to live. *German immigrant.*

Liberated in Canada

I felt so terribly hemmed in, in Sweden. So many possibilities weren't open to me — I couldn't do this because my family wouldn't like it, I couldn't do that because society wouldn't approve. I couldn't talk about making money, because that was vulgar . . . oh, I was liberated by coming here. *Swedish immigrant.*

No Room for Two Women

I can't remember Joe ever telling me he had a farm. Just where we were going to live, how we were going to make a living — I never thought about it. I only knew him for about two months before we were married on December 31, 1945. I was seventeen, the oldest of eight, and I'd worked since I was fourteen, in the Treasury Department in Whitehall. I was a filing clerk, and I made the tea. I met Joe at the Assembly of God Church in East Grinstead. I wanted so badly to get away from home — there were all these little ones around, and we never had any money.

Joe had this little farm in the Rainy River district of Northern Ontario, and I'd no idea how isolated it was going to be. It was a quarter section, and his mother had kept it up for him while he was away. She was a widow, and he was very close to her, and I wasn't prepared for that relationship. She didn't recognise our marriage, she didn't even send us a telegram. When my husband met me off the train in Winnipeg, it was August, the middle of the haying season, and my mother-in-law never forgave me for arriving then.

She lived with us for a year, and she ignored me most of the time, although sometimes she'd shout. There was the day the threshers were there, that first summer, and she was baking pies, and I forgot to put wood on the stove. She certainly shouted that day. But most of the time, she just ran things the way she always had. I'd get up early to help, but she'd be up even earlier. Finally, I went out into the field to pick rocks, and I was so pleased with myself. I felt I'd done something at last.

I was so lonely, I had to have a baby. My hus-

Ontario farmer.

band said it was like a toy to me. Joan was born in 1947, but I was very, very ill with toxemia beforehand. My mother-in-law was such a hard woman, she thought there was nothing to having babies, it was just like calves and baby pigs.

After a year, my husband and his brother bought her a little house in town. She never got over that, but I still believe there's no room for two women in one small house.

We lived like the pioneers did, and that was quite something after London. We had no running water, no electric light, and there was a wood-burning stove in the kitchen. We had coal oil lamps, until we graduated to gas lanterns. Instead of a fridge, we had a flowing well, with a cage in it. We canned our own meat and packed it in sealers, and hung it from the cage in the well, along with the milk and the baby's formula.

Until Joan was two, I washed on a washboard on the stoop, but I was the first person in the district to have a gasoline washing machine. We hung clothes out all winter. They froze, and the corners broke off where I pegged them, until I learned to hang the whole towel or sheet over the line.

At Christmas 1946, it was 50 degrees below [fahrenheit], and my husband put some logs in the oven to heat them up, to put our feet on, in the cutter. We drove the horses three miles over the snow, to visit some relatives. We were all bundled up in sheepskins. My children never believe me when I tell them about it. Later, we had a car, one of the very few in the district.

When I came to Canada, I thought I'd seen the last of my own family. I didn't realise how easy it would be to go home. In 1953, I went back with my daughter, and I took a one-way ticket because I thought I might stay. But my mother told me plainly, she had six daughters at home, and she couldn't look after me. So back I came.

Some people came to Canada for a better life. Well, that certainly wasn't true of me. It took me years and years to become a Canadian. I was a most unhappy person for a few years, but I'm resilient.

We made a sort of living on that farm for a few years, although my husband had to take on out-side jobs, like highway construction, from time to time. We were satisfied with much less then. I wasn't too good at milking cows, but I kept chickens and I learned to stook grain — it's very prickly, but I liked it. I don't remember ever being close to an animal till I got here, and I was terrified of horses, but I got over that. I was tougher than I thought I was. *English warbride.*

Homesickness

I didn't feel homesick the first year, everything was so new and different, but when my first child came, I thought a lot about home. We'd been a large, warm family and we were always together, grown-ups and children. Here, I was all by myself with the baby, while my husband worked. I'd find myself walking downtown with the baby, peering at people's faces — I was dying to see a familiar face, and the winter seemed so long. I used to watch for the snow to melt, every day from the beginning of January. Finally, in March, I wrote home to my parents, saying, "At last! I saw some ground today!"

Six years after I came here, I got a letter from my mother, saying she'd been ill and she was afraid she would never see me again. When I told my husband, he said, "You'll be on a boat next spring," and he took an extra job, moving furniture at night, to buy the ticket. I told my five-year-old, "We're going home to Wales," and he didn't understand what I was talking about.

By the time I actually left, my mother had recovered. We had a long visit, but after four months in Wales, I couldn't wait to get back. *Welsh warbride.*

A Corner to Call Our Own

The farmer who sponsored us had been to school with my father, in the same village. He came to Canada in the 1920s, and we thought he must be rich by now. In our dream of Canada, everybody lived in big houses, near wide highways lined with trees.

When we arrived in Tomahawk, we found my father's friend and his family living in a one-room cabin, a converted chicken coop, with no windows, and for two weeks we slept there too, nine people in a cabin, twelve feet by fifteen. There was no room between the beds.

These Tomahawk farmers were such poor people. Most were from eastern Poland or the Ukraine, and they'd come here twenty years before. They felt exploited and bitter, and some were very socialistic, even communistic.

There was no work for us in Tomahawk, and after two weeks my parents decided to move to Edmonton. There would be jobs there, somewhere, my father said. He did people's gardens for a while, and eventually he found a job in the steel industry. My mother washed dishes in a restaurant, twelve hours a day.

I was put into Grade 9, in Edmonton, in 1948, and I found it tough, because English didn't come that easily. I worked very hard to catch up, and then I started to move ahead of the others, and there was jealousy among my classmates. I didn't fit in very well with the other kids because I had a job at the Coca Cola bottling plant every day after school, from four to midnight, so there was no time for sports or extra-curricular activities, so I missed out on all the things teenagers did, like skating and skiing. Three weeks before exams, I took time off from the plant to study. I was washing Coca Cola bottles, and before I got there two people had fed this machine. But when I arrived, I did the job alone for 75¢ an hour. So there was resentment at the plant about immigrants always working harder than other people. That was a pretty general resentment around Edmonton, we found.

The truth is, we worked so hard to gain security. We had this tremendous urge to get a roof over our heads, because for eight years we'd never had one, and we were never sure where the next meal was coming from. Everybody in the family worked for this common goal, to have a corner of Canada to call our own. My father worked, my mother worked, my brother and I worked after school, and in two years he had the downpayment on our house. And then my mother took in boarders, five of them, for about six years, and my brother and I slept in the dining room.

In 1948, if people heard you speak your own language on a bus, or on the street, they would resent it, and sometimes they'd say straight out, "Why don't you speak English?" Slavs were regarded as ignorant, because the earlier immigrants had come as peasants, labourers. They couldn't read or write and their status was low here. We were treated the same, to begin with, and sometimes it came to blows and bloody noses.

But we were determined to establish ourselves, and once we had got the roof over our heads, the thing we wanted most was the car. First it was an old one, but in 1952 we got a navy blue Ford, super-duper, with white-wall tires, a Crestline, the top of the class. We drove it to Church on Sunday, my brother and I like young gentlemen in navy blue suits, and Mother in her fur, a black Persian

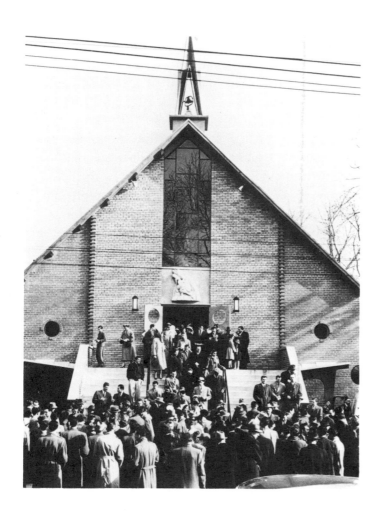

Our Lady Help of Christians Church, Toronto, was built by the Slovenian community, and blessed by Cardinal McGuigan, 1954.

lamb with a Nehru cap. Polish people always dress to kill, and we must have looked like a million dollars.

Our church was the anchor for so many people. It was our cultural center, as well as the place we went to worship. You went there to meet other Polish people, and that was where I met my future wife. Both our parents pushed us to seek out mates from the same stock, the same cultural, religious background. "There are so many things in life which separate you," they said. "You have these things in common to keep you together."

You feel so much pride and security when you get your Citizenship papers. My parents kept saying, "You kiss the soil of this big land. The German boot will never walk over it." But somehow, in spite of what they felt, my parents did not adapt well. Father was forty-eight and Mother was forty-three when we came, and they never learned to speak much English. At the steel plant, there were always other immigrants to talk to my father in Polish or German, and my mother stayed at home, looking after boarders who were immigrants too. Now, their old age is sad. We have stayed close to them, but they are cut off from so many things. They can't talk to their grandchildren, they can't even enjoy television or radio. They have no financial worries at all, but they are very lonely, and we worry about them. *Polish immigrant, Edmonton.*

Our Life is Here

My father was a bulb grower with an acre patch, and I was number three son. There was no way to split up a landbase so small.

I'd done two years in the army, and I wanted adventure. There was a long waiting list for California, and I was impatient, so I applied to Canada and I was accepted instantly. The Dutch government paid most of my fare.

When I went for my interview in The Hague, I told the immigration officer I wanted to go to British Columbia. "I'm a bulb grower," I said, "I need a warm climate, near the sea." Well, he said, unemployment was high in B.C., and either I went elsewhere in Canada, or nowhere at all. So I said I'd go to the other coast, without knowing anything about it. I was told I'd have to work for a farmer for one year and then I was on my own.

I landed at Halifax, and they sent me up to Milville, to a dairy farm with twelve cows. It was so backward I couldn't believe it, and yet they were so well off! They had a roomy house, central heating, a deep freeze, a big kitchen, bacon and eggs every day for breakfast. We Dutch people, we analyse everything, and I said to myself, "Things must come easier here, after Holland."

I didn't stay on that farm, as I was supposed to. I got offered a job as a greenskeeper-landscaper on a golf course, for $90 clear, and that was a whole lot better than $55 a month. I did odd jobs for a while after that, and then I bought a half-ton truck and became my own boss as a landscaper. I hired six immigrants to work for me, and I also rented a farm and worked that too. I never grew bulbs in Cape Breton, of course, that's impossible. I took up chicken farming. I saved every penny from the farm and from my landscape business, to build up a little capital and get started on my own land. In the wintertime, I made a little extra by selling Fuller brushes.

I was taken by the beauty of the country, the cows in the pastures under the trees, just like Switzerland. I wanted my own place so badly. At agricultural high school, I was taught to look for quality of soil, proximity to market, etc., but I didn't look for any of those things. I saw this farm on a beautiful March day, with the fields all covered with snow, fifty or sixty acres cleared, which was a lot for a Cape Breton farm, and I fell in love with it. It was for sale for $9,000 and I only needed 10% downpayment, because Nova Scotia was offering special incentives to attract Dutch farmers. You don't get breaks like that today.

We were brought up a certain way, to be thrifty, but to gamble too. You borrow money, but you pay your bills. I gambled and I worked hard and I've been a success. I married a Dutch girl I met here, and we've brought up a big family. I've done all the things that I wanted to when I came here.

We Dutch don't hang on to our customs, like some groups do . . . and yet I've never felt completely accepted, acclimatised. Our kids, though, they're 100% Canadian, they don't even speak Dutch. But that means our kids can't talk to their grandparents, and that bothers me. I know I sacrificed my own close family ties when I came here. I missed the old country a lot, but I was too stubborn and proud to admit it. Oh, we've been back many times on holiday, and we know it wouldn't be easy to fit in anymore. There are too many changes, and we've changed too much ourselves. Our life is here, with our children. *Dutch immigrant.*

Dutch farm family, Wolfe Island, Ontario, 1951.

Marriage

In 1947, my husband came to China to look for a wife. He was twenty-seven. An intermediary arranged for him to meet my parents, but they didn't tell me what was happening. One day they said, "Don't come home today." When I went back, there were lots of cookies, a celebration. They told me I was engaged. I felt very strange, and I cried, but that was the way it was then. My parents said, "This boy comes from Canada, he must have lots of money." But I never met him until the day I was married.

When I was two months pregnant, my husband left for Canada. My first baby was a boy, and my husband wrote to say how happy he was. In 1949, he wrote me a letter, sending me money and saying I was to get out to Hong Kong. I lived there one and a half years, and my boy was four when we sailed for Canada.

When I heard people talking English, it was just like birds on a tree, and I thought, "Oh my God, how will I manage?" The first years in Winnipeg were really hard, but my little boy was such a help. One day I'll never forget, it was winter and I was pregnant. I fell down in my big fur coat and my boy said, "Take it easy, Mummy, I'll help you." And when I cried he said, "Mum, Mum, don't cry. Shame on you!"

I'd been in Winnipeg a year, and I spoke not one word of English when my next baby was born. I went to a hospital, and they took my baby away as soon as she was born. The nurse told me my baby was okay, but I didn't understand. I waited and waited until my husband came, I was so frightened. But he explained, and then I was happy.

We moved to Newfoundland, and my husband opened a restaurant in St. John's. We have seven children now, but there are not many Chinese people here. My oldest boy married a Newfoundland girl. But my husband said, "You should marry one of your own people." He told me, "Don't you go to the wedding." Later, I went to our Chinese Church to pray, and I looked around, and I thought of my son getting married in another church, and no one there from his own family, no mother, no father, no brothers, no sisters, and I cried. I should have gone. *Chinese immigrant.*

Winnipeg, 1940s.

Vancouver, 1951

"... neither fish nor fowl."

I came to Toronto when my year on the railway was over, and I got into the College of Art. I had some money saved from the railway, and I got a small bursary. When the money ran out, I put myself through by working in a chocolate factory, from four till midnight. In those days I seemed to have endless energy.

After thirty years in Canada, I'm convinced that anyone can make it here, if you're young and healthy and determined — as long as you can survive the first few years. To start with, I was full of "go," but depression hit me when I got a job and started to do well. I had these same, awful nightmares, night after night, about trying to escape over the border into Austria. Yet I didn't have these dreams when I was working on the railway, only when I was in a good bed and a good house in Toronto.

During that bad time, I went to see an old friend who'd had a nervous breakdown, and I found that 90% of the patients [in the institution] were Europeans. This is maybe one side of the immigrant story that doesn't get told.

When I think back to those days, I can see we were slugging it out alone, with no family to fall back on, and nowhere to cry. My God, it wasn't easy. But the pressure eased up, gradually, as the years went by.

I got married, and I'm close to my family. There's no gap between me and my children, as there is in some immigrant families. I know that I belong here, though not in the same way my children do. I think I'm neither fish nor fowl. I went back to see my home in Yugoslavia thirty-two years after I left, and it was a real shock. I was a foreigner in my own land. People would ask me, "How come you speak Slovenian so well?" and I'd say, "I was born here." *Slovenian immigrant.*

Canadian Strangers became Family

I was an orphan when the war ended. I'd been in a concentration camp, and I was brought to France with some other survivors. I was sixteen at the time. I came from Roumania, where it joins the Ukraine.

Many of us came out of the concentration camps with a chip on our shoulder, a feeling that the world owed us a living. Intellectually, we didn't admit this, but deep down I think we felt it.

I didn't want to be a burden to some distant relatives I had in France. I couldn't stand the thought of some long-lost family giving me charity. I was naive, I guess, but I was young. When I heard about this scheme to send groups of orphans to Canada, I asked to go. My French relatives were opposed, but I had no qualms about accepting charity from total strangers. I planned to finish high school there, learn English, and then go back to Europe.

What I didn't think about was that these Canadian strangers who took me into their home would become familiar — that they would become my family. But they did. I came from a medical family, and Jewish Immigrant Aid Services placed me with a medical family in Toronto. They had children of their own, an older boy, an engineer, who was away from home, and a daughter, one year younger than me. We understood each other from the word go, and we're still good friends. But I was so lucky. Out of the group of sixteen or seventeen who came to Toronto, only two of us stayed with the original family.

We were difficult kids, and we came from many different backgrounds. We were older teenagers, not babies, and we'd been damaged by our war experiences, some of us very badly. It was hard to fit in, and after Europe, Toronto was so very provincial, so Waspy and dour. It was wet and dull when we arrived in October, and I remember thinking, "This is the ugliest city I've ever seen," all these semi-detached houses, in ugly red brick. Only Union Station had something familiar, in its massiveness. We went first to a house at College and Harbord, which JIAS had rented, and this old lady showed us around, so that we'd know how Canadians lived. She showed us a flush toilet, as if we'd never seen one before.

I had missed seven years of school, I spoke no English, and I had a very tough time indeed at Forest Hill Collegiate. It wasn't just the work and the language, it was the way we were supposed to behave, rules that didn't make sense. Some of our group from Europe were there too, and one day I tapped an old friend on the shoulder, and said to him, "Let's have lunch." I got reported for chasing boys, and the principal reprimanded me in front of everybody. I didn't understand what he said, or even what I'd done, but I thought he meant I was to pack up and leave, so I did just that. It took a while to sort that situation out.

I felt like an oddball. My hair was long and I wore it loose, and people were really bothered by that — they wanted me to tie it. In Europe, we washed and showered, but we didn't use deoderants, and we didn't shave our arms and legs, and that upset people too. If you wore sandals and jeans in the summer, people would stare.

You were supposed to wear a skirt, and stockings — and white gloves if you went anywhere special. You'd go into Eatons, and people would look at you as if you'd come from another planet, and as soon as you opened your mouth, they'd ask why you spoke funny. You just didn't hear accents in public places.

My family decided that no other language than English would be spoken at home, and they also decided that I shouldn't see too much of the kids I'd come with. Most of them left high school anyway, because they couldn't hack it. My family wanted me to meet new people, Canadians, and one way to do this, they told me, was to go to summer camp. Well, I went to pieces over that word. No way was I going to CAMP again, for the rest of my life! They were patient, they didn't push me, but the second summer I did go to camp, as a counsellor. They were right. I did make friends, and that's where I met my future husband.

At school, I started out in Grade 11, and with some extra help in English, I graduated two and a half years later. I applied for pre-meds at the University of Toronto, but I wasn't accepted. Being female *and* Jewish, I didn't make the quota. But my family phoned all the other medical schools, and I got into Western.

As it happened, I didn't finish my course, because I got married after a couple of years. But I was so fortunate to have all that help and support from my family in Toronto. I look back now on the way I came to Canada to live with these complete strangers — I could never do that again. I don't know how I did it. *Roumanian Jewish war orphan.*

Troubled Past

I changed my name after my son was born, and I got a lot of criticism from my family. But I don't want him to go through what I did. Nobody could pronounce Luciano, and certainly not my last name, and I got labelled as Italian. My parents still have a feeling for their mother country, despite the way they were treated, but I have never thought of myself as Italian.

For so many years, I haven't said anything about this, but I'm not proud of my heritage. My family came from Trieste, from an area which became Italian in 1920. It had been part of the Austro-Hungarian Empire, but my parents grew up in the 1930s, as Italians. Father was a hairdresser and Mother was a seamstress. They were both in Mussolini's youth movement, and my father fought for Mussolini all through the war. Yet the Germans shot my mother's family in 1944, because they thought they were partisans. And after the war, when Trieste became part of Yugoslavia, nobody wanted us. The Italians didn't care what happened. We were just DPs.

I was very small at the time, and I don't remember much about what happened then, but we were sent to a camp near Hamburg, and there were hundreds of women and children there. The men were sent ahead, to Canada. Canada was the only country which would take us, and I'm very grateful to this day.

The women and children stayed in the camp for nearly two years, until the men established themselves, and mostly we lived on bread and potatoes. My mother sold nearly everything we'd brought from Trieste to buy extra food, when she could, and when we finally came to Canada, we left with just five suitcases. My mother felt so guilty about the way I'd been fed, she couldn't put enough food into my mouth. She discovered America when she found Loblaws, and she went overboard, making up for all the eggs and butter and milk I'd missed. I have a weight problem to this day.

My father got a job at the Bata shoe factory, near Trenton, and that's where we lived for the first few years. He wasn't earning very much, about $25 a week, but every Friday, just like clockwork, I was sent to the post office in Trenton to mail a cheque back to my grandmother. Five years later, they brought her over, and the excitement, the anticipation were indescribable.

When we moved to Toronto, my father got a job on the assembly line at the Ford Motor Company, and he's still there. My mother worked in a chocolate factory on Spadina, making Sweet Marie bars. Now she's a housekeeper. They have been living in Toronto all these years, but in their hearts, they've been living in 1930s Italy. They wouldn't permit English in the home, unless it was on television. Outside, you spoke English, but inside you spoke Italian. We've never spoken English to my parents, not even my brothers, who were born here.

Every Saturday morning, my father took me and my brothers into the living room, and made us stand up to listen to records of Mussolini's speeches. You could see the ecstasy on his face. And he cut our hair military-style. He ruled us with an iron fist, and he wouldn't allow us to argue with him. He'd hit us if we tried. He'd left everything he'd known behind, and he couldn't stand being challenged in his own family.

We don't get on. I couldn't accept their values. In their view, you have to respect people with money, no matter how they made it. The important thing is to put money aside, to buy a house. My duty, as the oldest son, was to support them. I was to move in, with my new wife, so that my mother could be Matriarch. I didn't move in, and my brothers have left home. My parents are getting to be old, sad people.

My wife's parents came at the same time, in the same circumstances, yet they've changed, they've adapted to Canada. So it's not just the age you come here that matters.

I'll tell you something that sounds contradictory, after what I've said. I'm grateful to my parents for insisting we spoke Italian at home. I think languages are important, and we speak Italian to our son. We think Italian will be useful to him, as a Canadian. *Italian immigrant.*

Italian immigrant family reunited, Union Station, Toronto.

"A very good wife . . . ."

My sister lied to me. She told me when she sponsored me, I would have a good job with this contractor in Sudbury, and for my first day at work, I put on my best suit, my gold watch and chain, and beautiful shoes. I had a certificate in land surveying in Italy, but I found that this job was a labourer's, making bricks, and I was not trained for that kind of job. My pride disappeared completely. In five months I had five different jobs, as a doughnut maker, as an oven man, as a janitor, as a labourer. I was lonely and unhappy, and I started to drink, far too much.

My sister said, "Why not go to Toronto and study some more?" The stupid thing was, I didn't go to school right away to learn English, and I had this sense of inferiority — I couldn't get a job because of the language. But I was scared to move, alone, to Toronto. I never liked a big city. I like a town where in five minutes you can reach the cinema, the grocery store. And it is like a protection to have a sister, one of my own family, in this place.

I was so lonely that after a year and a half I went back to Italy to find a girl to marry me, a girl from my own town who would understand me. I got engaged to a beautiful girl, but she said she did not want to marry me so soon, to go to Canada. She said to me, "Go back and see if you are happy there, and if you are, then I will come to you. And if you are miserable, come home, and then we will marry."

So I came back to Sudbury, and things started to go well for me. I studied basic English, I took a course in drafting at night school, and I got a job I liked. Then I married my wife. We were married by proxy. That means I must bring four witnesses before the Italian vice-consul to say I'm not married in Canada, then I send a proxy by the priest here to the parish priest in Italy. My father-in-law took my wife to the church, in her wedding dress, for the marriage ceremony, and the priest read out my responses. You must imagine our wedding night. I was in Sudbury and she was in Calabria.

My wife came, and she was wonderful, though she suffered very much from the cold. Like me, she dreamed of a rich country, big houses, beautiful clothes. Sudbury was not like her dream. But she is a very good wife. We had little money, but she could cook with one dollar, or she could cook with ten, and always my shirts were clean. She is the mother of two Canadian children, good children, and I teach them to respect their parents, to speak our language at home. One goes to university, one is at school, and my only fear is for the future. There will not be much work for them in Sudbury, where will they live? It is very important for me to have my family all together.

But that is the future. Now, our life is good. It is not the America of the movies, but money is not everything. *Italian immigrant, Sudbury.*

At the Back of the Bus

There was no black community in Ottawa, at that time, and dating wasn't easy. My sister and I were quite good at dancing, and people would ask us to parties, to warm things up, but that was all there was to it. It was especially difficult for my sister. A black girl might be attracted to somebody white, but he had to be man enough to take her out, to step out of line from his friends.

For me, it was easier, because I worked in a lab, and most people in labs were female in those days. There was a fair amount of prejudice, but on the whole women are much less prejudiced than men. Some of them went out with me. They could always use the excuse, "We work at the same place."

When I started going steady with a girl from Hull, her mother used the same kind of excuses. She owned a little store, and when people asked her, "Is Louise serious about him?" she'd say, "Oh no, no, no. He's a good customer at the store, and he's a member of the church bowling team."

Sometimes, prejudice came right out in the open. One Sunday afternoon I was window shopping on Rideau Street with my girl friend and her sister, and suddenly this car pulled up. Four doors opened, and six men jumped out and blocked the sidewalk. I guess seeing me, a black man with two blonde ladies, got them mad. They didn't say anything; they just stood there. "Just keep on walking," I said to my girl friend. We got closer and closer and then, when we were about four yards from them, they jumped back in the car and took right off. But if we'd stopped, or turned round, they would have beaten me up, for sure.

Jamaican immigrants.

On the bus to Ottawa every day, people would stare at me so much I'd feel uncomfortable, so I sat right at the back. I wondered, at first, "Why are they looking at me? Oh gee, it's because they think I'm different." But I knew, inside, that I just *looked* different.

Then one sunny day I was going down Sparks Street, and there was a reflection of this strange-looking person in a store window. I spun round. I said, "There's another black man in town!" and there was nobody there but me. I was a stranger in town. I felt it myself.

Being stared at on those buses really got to me after two years. I promised myself, when I can afford a car, I'll never take another bus in my life. And I didn't, for seventeen years. *Jamaican immigrant.*

Money Can Buy Happiness

My brother-in-law is a very successful man. He's a leader in our local community, and he doesn't want people to know about my sister's early beginnings in Canada. But for myself, I don't care. We had it rough, but it's okay now.

We lived very comfortably in Beirut. My dad and his brother owned a restaurant, and my mother had a maid for us kids, a woman to do the laundry, and a waiter from the restaurant used to bring us breakfast, lunch and supper, and pack up all the dirty dishes afterwards. The restaurant was open twenty-four hours a day, and when his brother left, it was too much for my father to manage. He sold the business, and he decided to come to Montreal and open a restaurant. My mother had four sisters there, and one of them sponsored us.

In the first six months, my father took sick. At first, they thought he had TB, and he was quarantined. But it was lung cancer, and all the money we'd brought went on my father's illness. There was no medicare, and we had no insurance. At the end, it cost $15 a day just to keep him in a hospital ward, in a room with twenty-three other people, and then there was the medicine. He lived three years. He was forty-eight when he died, and my mother had four kids: I was nine, my brother was seven, and my two sisters were sixteen and eighteen.

We didn't get help from anyone. My aunts never offered, and my parents were too proud to ask. My mother went to work in a factory, making lingerie, and so did my two older sisters. They all made between $23 and $27 a week.

My mother worked from 8:00 a.m. to 6:00 p.m., then she would go to the hospital to see my father. I got my brother and me ready for school, and when we came home, I was in charge. I was the cook. I was ten or eleven years old.

I went to work in the same factory as my mother, and I lied about my age. I was fourteen, but I was mature-looking, and I said I was seventeen. I never worked on a machine, but I gave work to the other girls. I lugged boxes and fetched thread, and I earned $13 a week. But I also went to night school, and got my diploma in shorthand and typing, and in 1961 I started working for a notary public, for $50 a week. I'll never forget that; it was $2,600 a year. Soon, I was earning more. I was quite bilingual. The whole family spoke French, but in Montreal I went to an English school. My father was Catholic, but he was not very religious, and he preferred us to go to the public school, to learn English.

My middle sister, who got married, was like Cinderella in the fairy story. When this man proposed to her, she couldn't refuse. He was a chartered accountant, and he came from a well-to-do family. He turned out to be the most wonderful husband, and he made her feel like a queen. They tell you money can't buy happiness, but to me that's baloney. After she married, she didn't have to work one more day in her life. *Lebanese immigrant.*

Knitting machines, Montreal.

My Own Family was Foreign to Me

My story is different, because I came to Canada many years after my parents. I was a baby when they left Poland during the war, and they left me behind with my grandparents. After the war, when they were in a refugee camp near Bremerhaven, they wanted me back, but my grandparents wouldn't let me go. They were afraid I might never reach them. So my parents left for Canada, as DPs, and for years after, the Polish government refused to issue me a passport. I was thirteen before I was allowed to leave Poland, and by then I didn't really want to go, to join these parents I didn't remember, and my younger sister who was born in Germany.

I flew to Montreal, and it was the most stunning, the most frightening thing, to arrive in this huge, lit-up area. I was never familiar with electricity in my village. I read my school books by coal oil lamps, and I remember thinking — it was all so disconnected — "Who could possibly pay for all this?" I can still see my mother standing in the passage at Dorval. I could recognise her face from pictures, but everything about her, and about my father, was totally strange. My sister looked so grown up, so American. I had this feeling that they were foreign, and yet they were my family.

I never did build up the close understanding some people have with their parents, and for a long time I wanted to go back, though after six months I realised that nothing would come of it. I wasn't able to cope with the language, and I couldn't eat the food my mother cooked. I was so hungry for potatoes and pork, the staple foods in Poland, but my mother didn't cook this familiar food. She left Poland at seventeen.

The biggest problem was not being able to reconcile what I'd been taught with what I found. I'd say things about capitalist societies having distinct groups of people who are rich and all the others poor, with nothing in between, and I would make people mad. I got into real fights with the roomer who lived with us, who spoke Polish, and he said I was "brainwashed." I was so furious, but I held on to my convictions. It took me a long time to think for myself.

All these differences in my background showed up in dozens of little ways. Like when my mother took me to buy a pair of waterproof boots on St. Lawrence, and she argued with the storekeeper over the price. I was so angry. I said, "You can't bargain, the government sets the price. Whatever the price indicates, you pay the full amount." These things sound small, but they made a gap between me and my family.

Life wasn't easy for my parents. My mother was a waitress and a cleaning lady, and my father worked on sewer construction, although he got to be a foreman with a good salary, after some years. Both of them said their children must have something better than they'd had, and they let us go to University. They helped us financially. Some Europeans wouldn't do that for girls, but my parents did. *Polish immigrant, Montreal.*

"I was never an outsider."

When I was first here, I'd be walking along a street and I'd say to myself, "This isn't real. This is a fantasy world, and I'm supposed to be somewhere else." I expect every immigrant has that feeling of unreality.

I was seventeen when my father came to work in Toronto. He was forty-five, and my mother was fifty-six, so according to all the rules they should have found it hard to adapt, but they didn't. They soon had their small, tight group of friends, and they settled down into a rhythm of life that still pertains. There was an incredible difference in our living standards. We'd come from a rented row house in Birmingham with an outside toilet, and our hot water system depended on lighting fires. Here, everything was new. The furniture, the house itself, even the car was nearly new. Father's salary could pay for it all.

It's more difficult to articulate the non-material things which were so attractive, the "unstuffiness," the freedom of opportunity. In 1953, in England, there was nothing in my lifestyle to encourage me to be anything but lower-middle-class. It was a very ordered society then, and there was a system of predestination involved that was very hard to break out of. There was no sense of revolt, of freedom, of radicalism — that came in the 1960s.

I came here at seventeen and I sensed that here, I had time to make up my mind what to do. There was an infinite range of possibilities, and I could do any damn thing I wanted. There were no limitations in Toronto, but when I went back to England, six or seven years later, I found a society full of limitations.

Scottish immigrants examine used car, Ottawa, 1955.

Toronto was a very traditional society, still, when we arrived. The great social changes hadn't happened in 1953, and the Protestant work ethic was alive and well in the suburb we lived in. But it wasn't a clannish society, and nobody cared that I hadn't been to school here. I was enormously fortunate that I could overcome the hurdle of entering society here by going to university, and I was never an outsider. Society made no assumptions about me, and I made none about it. *English immigrant, Toronto.*

"Just like the pioneers."

Canada has been good to me because I made it so. Just as the old pioneers had to fight against the elements, so I had to fight against other elements — professional discrimination and hostility. For we doctors were not accepted very kindly after the war. Canadian doctors actually said things like, "Why didn't you stay in Europe? We don't need you here."

I'm proud of my heritage. I come from a family that's 700 years old, and I took my medical degree at the second oldest university in Europe, Charles University in Prague. I interned in Czechoslovakia, and again in a refugee camp hospital in Germany, after the Communist Putsch. But none of this counted in Canada. To be fair, it would have been difficult in any of the other countries I enquired about.

I had to start as an orderly in a Catholic hospital in Victoria, and it was impossible to get an internship in British Columbia. The College of Physicians and Surgeons wouldn't recognise my diploma, and finally I was taken on by an Ontario hospital. I got my licence, thank God, but afterwards, when I wanted to do postgraduate training in surgery, there was no way I could break into the system, as an immigrant. I had to go to England to specialise, and then I came back to Canada as a surgeon.

My approach is very different from those immigrants with the backdoor open — people from England, for instance. I couldn't go back. There is no way a political refugee can go back. So your mind is set: here you are in this country, and here you must make good. And you do, despite all the difficulties. Just like the pioneers. *Czech immigrant.*

"Canada has been good to us . . . ."

I started working in a chicken cannery for 45¢ an hour, and then I moved over to B.C. Packers. They paid better, 80 or 90¢. It was cold work. I was packing frozen fish for the stores to sell, but I was helping my family to live a little better, and I worked there eighteen years.

One thing, though — that job didn't help me with the English language. There were lots of other immigrants there, so many nice people, but so many different nationalities, and none of us knew much English.

In his work, my husband had the same experience. In engineering, you have your books and tables. You don't need to speak English too much. He understood his superiors, and they understood him, and that was enough.

We haven't many friends outside our own community in Vancouver. Maybe that's because of language, but maybe it's our own fault. We brought our family with us when we came, and there were other Latvians here already in this city. We've all stayed close to each other and to other Scandinavians. We went to a Swedish church when we first arrived.

Did we do the right thing, coming here? We ask ourselves about it, as we grow older. We go back to Europe on visits, and it seems closer, even now. Our Latvian friends who stayed in Sweden after the war have done well. They've settled in more than we have here. But Canada has been good to us, and to our daughter. We have all the things we wanted, that we worked hard for. *Latvian immigrant.*

Salmon cannery, British Columbia.

"_. . . your wildest dreams._"

My uncle kept on writing, saying, "Come on over. Here you can fulfill your wildest dreams." I decided to come for a year, but I loved it from day one, and it never crossed my mind to go back.

I was a young fellow, twenty-four, with no family, no responsibilities — those things change people. I was cocksure, I knew my trade as a machinist, and I got a job with the railway in Manitoba. I only knew a few words of English, and I was maybe stupidly sure of myself. It never crossed my mind that I could be unemployed. I suppose I knew that my uncle was working, and he would feed me if I was in trouble.

I worked on the nightshift, for the railway, and I started building houses on the side. My dream was to make enough money to start my own company. I'd saved $2,200 and I spent it all on a building lot. A friend said to me, "Ernie, you'll lose your shirt," and I said, "So what?" I was young and carefree. You can never replace that feeling.

I didn't have these terrible fears of a Depression that Canadians had: "Is it going to be this year? Or next year? Then maybe the year after that?" That's how people thought, when I got here. They couldn't forget the 1930s.

All this time, I'd been writing to a girl I'd met in Germany, and I brought her to Canada at Christmas, 1952. We had to be married within four weeks, because she came as a bride. That was the rule. A real shotgun wedding, you might say.

It was easy for us to live cheaply here, because we were used to having so little. Canadians didn't realise that for years we'd had meat only twice a week. So here, we had meat three times a week, and it was a big improvement. My wife wrote back to Europe to tell people how well, how beautifully we ate. "In Germany," she said, "we ate a bowl of potatoes and a little piece of meat. Here, we have a huge piece of meat, with the potatoes hiding behind it."

We bought everything in bulk — 100 pounds of flour, oil in gallon drums, pork bellies to make our own fat. In the late 1950s, when my business was doing nicely, I remember my accountant throwing up his hands when I told him my wife fed our family on $15 a week. All the money I made, everything, went back into my business. I went to work on a bike, a lady's bike, with a toolbox on the back — my wife brought it with her from Europe. It was an old war-time bike. Finally, when I bought a car, I paid cash for it. It was a Pontiac station wagon, the cheapest big car on the market. I could put my tools in it.

All immigrants have rough experiences, and I'll let other people tell you about those. Many people went through hell the first few years, because of the unknown, because of the language barriers. The older people, who'd been through the war, they were burned much more than young men like myself. I have my own horror stories, and I wouldn't have missed one of them, because of what they taught me. Canada has been good to us. We've been lucky. We were young and we were healthy — that's important. And we built a foundation before building the rest. _Ethnic German, from Russia._

X   Conclusion:
Changes in the Old Order

Night school language classes for New Canadians,
Toronto, 1955.

IN THE 1950s, RETURNING PROSPERITY in northwest Europe was beginning to dry up some of the traditional sources of immigration, at a time when the demand for immigrant labour continued to run high in Canada. The mid-fifties marked the end of a period when "the problem was one of selection rather than recruitment, and services could be kept down to the minimum requirements of processing," as pointed out by the Citizenship and Immigration Department's submission to the Royal Commission on Canada's Economic Prospects. "Except in the Mediterranean area," the submission continued, "where Canada's bargaining position remains strong, the refugee and overpopulation problems have lost their character of emergency."

Unskilled labourers from the traditionally "non-preferred" southern European countries arrived in large numbers, and these numbers escalated because of the government's family-oriented immigration policy, which allowed Canadian citizens and residents to sponsor relatives. By the mid-1950s, says immigration specialist Freda Hawkins, "it was calculated that one Italian immigrant meant forty-nine Italian relatives, and the potential for family sponsorship was even higher." Family-oriented immigration in the 1950s and early 1960s changed the social make-up of Canada before the rules of entry were rewritten by the Pearson government in 1967.

By 1955, 26% of Toronto's population was of neither British nor French background, and in Edmonton and Winnipeg the proportion was 37% and 45%, respectively. (In Montreal it was only 14%). As newcomers arrived, Canadians were departing in significant numbers. Between 1945 and 1958, 425,000 Canadian citizens emigrated to the United States, but it is not known how many of these people were born in Canada, and how many were naturalised citizens.

Despite the increasing diversity of the population, there was little ethnic conflict in Canadian cities in the 1950s. What David Corbett referred to as "a remarkable decline in racial and national prejudice" on the part of the labour unions was partly due to high employment, and partly to the fact that second and third generation non-Anglo-Saxons were now becoming visibly upwardly mobile, in the union movement, as elsewhere. The barriers of class were being broken, and the process was helped by what Howard Palmer called the "collapse of the intellectual underpinnings of Anglo-Saxon superiority," which accompanied the decline of Britain as a world power.

It is interesting to find that, between October 1953 and October 1954, 273 physicians, trained outside Canada, passed their Canadian examinations. While 155 of them were from Britain and twenty from the United States, two "preferred" sources, the other ninety-eight were from Europe and Asia.

Along with class barriers, religious barriers were crumbling too, as old animosities between Protestants and Roman Catholics lost their significance. Nonetheless, Immigration Minister J.W. Pickersgill took evasive action when asked a loaded question in the House of Commons in 1955, as to whether immigrants were admitted in "rough proportion" to existing religious faiths. (The questioner was really seeking information about the number of Catholic immigrants entering Canada.) Pickersgill replied that he would consider any such selection "reprehensible," although he admitted that newcomers were asked to state their religious affiliation on arrival. But no statistics were tabulated from this information. "To be quite frank about it," said Pickersgill, "they might be a source of dispute, conflict and dissension in this country."

In Quebec, opposition to large-scale immigration continued throughout this period. In the early 1950s, Quebec newspapers and Ottawa's clerico-nationalist *Le Droit* both expressed anxiety about preserving the "ethnic balance," whereby French Canadians represented 30.8% of the population. "As in previous years, the immigration question provokes nothing but a purely negative reaction," said *Le Soleil* in August 1952, "because, inevitably, the huge majority of immigrants does not come from our ethnic group and cannot be assimilated into it." However, *Le Soleil* went on to acknowledge that some French and Belgian immigrants were among the newcomers, and efforts should be made to help them adjust. In that same week, *Le Droit* acknowledged that "now we must make immigration work for our interests, our birthrate is not enough." Almost two years earlier, *Le Canada* suggested that "a traditionally cold-hearted attitude to immigration on the part of too many French Canadians is driving away Catholics with whom it would be comparatively easy to make friends and allies."

One of the ironies of Canadian history is that, while Quebec was traditionally opposed to large-scale immigration, a French Canadian prime minister, Louis St. Laurent, presided over the major wave of immigration into postwar Canada. Another French Canadian prime minister, Sir Wilfrid Laurier, had held office during the first great turn-of-the-century wave. Both men happened to be in power during periods of rapid economic expansion, and both recognised that immigration was essential to the process.

Attitudes to immigration were changing during the 1950s, and a more humanitarian approach to refugees became apparent. In 1956, Immigration Minister Pickersgill arranged free passage for 37,000 Hungarians who fled their country after the Revolution. And two years later, in World Refugee Year, the Diefenbaker Conservative government modified immigration regulations to allow over 11,000 refugees to enter Canada, many of whom were ill or disabled.

Pressures to end Canada's traditional preference for British and northwest European immigrants began to be felt in the 1950s, and in 1962, the Diefenbaker government introduced immigration regulations designed to remove the earlier racial bias. Five years later, the Pearson Liberal regime introduced a new nondiscriminatory "point system" for assessing immigrants, according to their education, training and personal qualities, as well as occupational demand.

"A national government dealing with immigration policy is like a ship buffeted by contrary winds," wrote David Corbett in 1957. "Labour blows one way, and employers another. French Canadians puff up a powerful blast, various nationality associations exert pressures, and a chill draught of prejudice comes from some of the old stock. In these gusty waters the government must steer a course. Sometimes it may choose to use its auxiliary motors and go against the wind." The "contrary winds" continued to blow with varying force in the years to come.

Acknowledgements

The people who really made this book possible are the former immigrants who were willing to talk to me, a stranger, about their personal experiences. It was agreed, at the outset, that I would not "name names," but my thanks go out to everyone I interviewed during my travels across Canada, between 1977 and 1979.

All the photographs advertising Canada to would-be immigrants come from National Film Board filmstrips, commissioned by the Immigration Branch of the Department of Citizenship and Immigration. I am particularly grateful to Floyd Elliott and Joe MacDonald of the Board's Multi-Media division for retrieving so much valuable material from the vaults, and for taking such a personal interest in this project.

The photographs of immigrants en route to Canada and after their arrival, along with additional photographs of Canada between 1945-1955, come from a wide variety of sources: from Canadian National and the Toronto Telegram photo collection at York University; from the Public Archives of Canada and the provincial archives of Ontario, Saskatchewan and Alberta; from Air Canada and Canadian Pacific; from Canadian Press; from the Multicultural History Society of Ontario; from the Glenbow-Alberta Institute; from libraries at Memorial University, Newfoundland and the University of New Brunswick; from Ontario Hydro, the Aluminum Company of Canada, and the Toronto Transit Commission, which all employed immigrant labour; from various churches and ethnic organizations involved in bringing immigrants to Canada and helping them settle here, including the Jewish Immigrant Aid Services, Canadian Lutheran World Relief, the Conference of Mennonites in Canada and the Roman Catholic Church. The Rev. William Sturhahn of the North American Baptist Church and the Rev. A. S. Murray of the United Church helped me find other photographs, and so did several private citizens, who very kindly searched their photo albums on my behalf. Many photographs had to be copied, and I am indebted to Mrs. Cipa Zilber for the exceptional care she took in reproducing them.

One immigrant artist who came to Canada as a Displaced Person showed me sketches he made while in a refugee camp, on board ship en route to Canada, and at work on the railway here. I want to thank Ted Kramolc for letting me use some of these drawings in my book.

Some of the photographs which should have been in this book were never actually taken, because of the lack of Canadian news photographers in Europe. Canadian Press relied upon American wire services, and their photographs naturally showed refugees being processed by American immigration officials, and boarding American ships bound for the United States. While some key newspaper collections are closed to researchers, many newspapers destroyed their photographs from this period, and so, alas, did Immigration Branch information officers, as they "updated" their picture files at the end of the 1950s.

Background material for this book came from the 1940s files of the Immigration Branch and the Department of Labour, now in the Public Archives of Canada, and from the Library of the Employment and Immigration Commission. Various people who were involved in developing public policy and administering it during the postwar years contributed to my understanding of the period. They included the Hon. J.W. Pickersgill, Personal Assistant to Prime Minister Mackenzie King and later Minister of Citizenship and Immigration in the St. Laurent government; the two deputy ministers responsible for immigration in the ten postwar years, Dr. Hugh Keenleyside and Col. Laval Fortier; and various department officials, including officers at the Port of Halifax and an information officer who worked in tandem with the National Film Board on the filmstrip series *Life in Canada*. Mr. Fenton C. Crosman, a former Inspector-in-Charge, Halifax, gave me access to his extensive newspaper clipping files.

Shaping all the material collected into publishable form was a difficult task, and I owe a great deal to the perception and patience of my editor, Ramsay Derry. Thanks also to Catherine Baker and to Joseph Solway who saw it through to production.

Recommended Reading

Books

Corbett, D. C. *Canada's Immigration Policy: A Critique.* Toronto: University of Toronto Press, 1957.

Dirks, Gerald E. *Canada's Refugee Policy. Indifference or Opportunism?* Montreal: McGill-Queen's Press, 1977.

Green, Alan G. *Immigration and the Postwar Economy.* Toronto: Macmillan, 1976.

Hawkins, Freda. *Canada and Immigration. Public Policy and Public Concern.* Montreal: McGill-Queen's Press. 1972.

Richmond, Anthony. *Postwar Immigrants in Canada.* Toronto: University of Toronto Press, 1970.

Timlin, Mabel F. *Does Canada Need More People?* Toronto: Oxford University Press, 1951.

Abella, Irving and Troper Harold. *None is Too Many. Canada and the Jews of Europe, 1933-1948.* Toronto: Lester and Orpen Dennys, 1982.

Periodicals and Dissertations

Abella, Irving and Troper, Harold. "The Line Must be Drawn Somewhere: Canada and Jewish Refugees, 1933-1939." *Canadian Historical Review,* Vol. LX, No. 2, June 1979.

Rawlyk, George A. "Canada's Immigration Policy, 1945-1962." *The Dalhousie Review*, Vol. 42, No. 3, Autumn 1962.

Palmer, Howard. *Nativism and Ethnic Tolerance in Alberta, 1920-1972.* Diss. York University, Toronto, 1973.